WRITTEN

WHO'S WHO IN NEW COUNTRY MUSIC

VAUGHAN

St. Martin's Press/New York

Picture credits:

Adrian Boot, Asylum, BMG Records, Byworth-Wootton
International, Capitol Records, CBS Records Inc, Curb Records,
Demon Records, Elektra, Epic Records, Featherbed Productions,
First Generation Records, Liberty Records, Buddy Lee
Attractions Inc, London Features International, MCA Records,
MGM Records, Monument, MTM Records, PBS, Pictorial Press,
Polygram Records, PT Records, RCA Records And Cassettes,
Tom Sheehan, Sincere Management, Sire Records, Special
Delivery, Top Billing, Warner Brothers Records.

Every effort has been made to trace the copyright holders of the
photographs in this book but one or two were unreachable. We
would be grateful if the photographers concerned would contact
us.

Acknowledgements

This book is dedicated to Jean.

Thanks to the following:
The press and publicity officers of MCA, RCA, CBS, Polygram,
WEA and EMI/Capitol, especially Martha Moore, Sandy Neese
and Rona Rubin.
The Country Music Association.
Pam Lewis, Trisha Walker and Kathy Gangwisch.
To Tony Brown and Gary Valetri for filling in the gaps.
To Ricky Skaggs, Emmylou Harris and Rodney Crowell for
reminiscing.
To Lena Lucas and her address book.
To Tony 'Hot Tub' Byworth and Richard Wootton for advice and
support.
To Frank 'Crayfish' Warren.
And especially to Jo and Kansas for patience.

Bibliography

Country Music USA, Bill C. Malone (University Of Texas Press).
Illustrated Country Almanac, Richard Wootton (Virgin).
Nashville, Music City, USA, John Lomax III (Abroms)

Magazines consulted include, *NME, Melody Maker, Q, Country
People, Journal Of Country Music, Music Row*.

Library of Congress Cataloging-in-Publication Data

Vaughan, Andrew.
    Who's who in new country music / Andrew Vaughan.
        p. cm.
  ISBN 0-312-03953-0
    1. Country music—Bio-bibliography. I. Title.
  ML 105. V25 1990
  781.642'092'2—dc20
  [B]   89-27126
                              CIP
                              MN

First published in Great Britain by Omnibus Press.
First U.S. Edition
10 9 8 7 6 5 4 3 2 1

WHO'S WHO IN NEW COUNTRY MUSIC
CONTENTS

FOREWORD

BY RICKY SKAGGS

I love what's going on in country music today. There's lots of good down-home sounds like I grew up with in Kentucky, and some pretty neat new people who are showing the world that country is a happenin' thing. Proof of that, at least in part, is the fact that in America there are 2,690 radio stations playing country music, more than play rock or pop or classical or any other type. And country is attracting thousands of new fans every year in the UK, as well as in dozens of countries around the world.

In the 1970's when I was playing with different bands – my own and Emmylou Harris' Hot Band for a time – I couldn't find much that I termed 'country roots' music on the radio. Around 1979 and '80, as I listened to what was coming out of Nashville, I heard more pop-flavoured songs than anything, and I felt a musical heritage was about to be lost. There didn't seem to be many artists standing up for the real traditions like our forefathers in country such as Flatt And Scruggs, Roy Acuff, George Jones, and some of my other heroes. I didn't set out to take country music back to its roots, because I didn't think I could. When I got my chance with Epic Records in 1981, I just went in the studio to cut an album of traditional country sounds. As it happened, I successfully combined bluegrass and country for the first time, but I wasn't trying to tear down any barriers. I simply made music the only way I knew how.

Now it's pretty amazing for me to see the swift changes that have taken place in our industry. People like Dwight Yoakam, Reba McEntire, The Judds, Ricky Van Shelton, Randy Travis and lots more are responsible for a whole new strength in country music. What I like are the wide audiences these people have brought with them. We all have our own personal musical styles that touch various portions of the listening public and awaken them to country. I've always liked different kinds of music: rock, jazz, R&B, but my heart is in country. These days, the heart of country music seems to be back in the older more traditional sounds, and the fans are telling us they like it. So many of the popular new artists are giving us a fresh approach to a time-honoured music, and that makes me proud.

Ricky Skaggs

5

INTRODUCTION

The mid-eighties have been boom times for country music. Ever since Ricky Skaggs proved that back-to-basics country could outsell cross-over pop country, Nashville has been alive with the sound of new acts. A plethora of artists from Dwight Yoakam to Nanci Griffith have not only surfaced but overshadowed a group of more established country stars who'd planned on long careers without too many challenges.

The sequined shackles are being cast aside as the spirit of Hank Williams once more runs through Nashville's veins. Not since the 'outlaw' days of Willie Nelson and Waylon Jennings has country music been taken so seriously outside the country media. Country music is hip. The rock press treat it with the same respect as jazz or blues, not with the derision of yesteryear.

Not long ago, when country went pop, the sound, in the words of Emmylou Harris . . . "had very little to do with country music. Some of it was so bland that it sounded more like elevator music to me." It was a desire to recapture the original essence of country music that united the new country or new traditionalist movement. Artists like Reba McEntire and Dwight Yoakam felt strongly that their musical heritage was being lost amid a chorus of synthesizers and drum machines.

Whereas the 'outlaw' artists concentrated on forging a new sound – a combination of country and rock – many of the new Nashville pickers, singers and poets are dedicated to preserving an old-time sound. For some, like Skaggs, it's the symbol of a better time, security in a more traditional lifestyle. For others, Yoakam in particular, new traditionalism is a means of updating a classic country sound and proving that hard country is as exciting, passionate and dynamic as rock music.

With one or two exceptions, none of the artists in the new wave of country appeared from nowhere. Many have been playing a roots country style for years but always on the fringes of the country music industry. Others have been playing the Nashville game, making the kinds of records necessary for success, but once freed by new attitudes towards hard country they have responded with a new style of music. Even Barbara Mandrell, so long the archetypal mainstream country pop performer, has gone back to basics, as have Tammy Wynette and Glen Campbell.

The list goes on. This is the proof of a movement. The new artists' success has worked its way into the music of mainstream Nashville. Music shop owners with stocks of fiddles and steel guitars must be dreaming of holidays in Hawaii. But new country did not just happen: the economics of the industry allowed a change to occur. After a slump in sales in the early eighties something had to rescue country from the doldrums. History pointed to a reassertion of the roots of country music, roots which had been almost forgotten when Nashville went pop.

Back in the late fifties when rock 'n' roll threatened country sales, Nashville came up with the strings-heavy 'Nashville Sound' and scored with a slew of cross-over pop hits from the likes of Patsy Cline and Jim Reeves. Artists like Roy Orbison and The Everly Brothers, both major influences on new country acts, recorded hits in Nashville and other, more individual country musicians – Johnny Cash, Merle Haggard, Buck Owens and Roger Miller – forged their own country path, making sixties country diverse and exciting. Twenty years later a similar diversity developed, this time with a broader base of influences and a wider potential market.

OPPOSITE:
EMMYLOU HARRIS

7

PATSY CLINE

While the music of many of Nashville's new artists has its roots in pre-rock 'n' roll country music (see the A-Z of classic country artists at the end of this book), its origin as an attitude and a music can best be located in the sixties. In Nashville, classic country was created by Patsy Cline, Roger Miller brought younger audiences into country, Roy Orbison used his awesome vocals to perfection on a number of Nashville records, Merle Haggard cut hard country, Johnny Cash did things his own way and a batch of great songwriters, notably Loretta Lynn, Dolly Parton and Tom T. Hall ensured country music kept pace with the dramatic changes in America's social make-up.

On the West Coast, musicians softened their sound with some country injections, eventually developing a full-blown country rock genre. And in Texas, a circle of country musicians who steadfastly refused to play by anyone's rules other than their own, created a thriving music community.

California took the lead. The booming singer/songwriter scene in LA attracted a host of young musicians, many of them with country backgrounds. Chris Hillman, for example, played mandolin in a bluegrass band long before he became a Byrd. Gram Parsons thought of little else but those old-time harmonies of The Louvins, and Texas songwriters like Michael Murphey and Mike Nesmith rode into LA with a twang in their voices and a country tune in their hearts.

While it's normally accepted that Gram Parsons was the most influential figure in the development of country rock, other artists were simultaneously working on their own fusion of country and rock 'n' roll. A set of threads and links can be drawn from The Byrds, through The Flying Burrito Brothers to Emmylou Harris, Ricky Skaggs and the new wave of country in the eighties. More of that later.

LINDA RONDSTADT
RIGHT: **MICHAEL NESMITH**

Back in 1965 when The Byrds were still playing folk-rock, another set of connections and coincidences began in Hollywood. It may seem bizarre to cite the pop group The Monkees as prime movers in the country rock trend but their importance was crucial. Guitarist Michael Nesmith had played with country combos in Texas before heading for LA and TV stardom, but prior to passing The Monkees' auditions he hosted Monday night hootenanny shows at the LA Troubadour, a hive of folkie activity where the likes of Stephen Stills, Linda Ronstadt and the nucleus of The Eagles tried out their songs. In 1965 Nesmith penned an up-tempo country-tinged rock song, 'Different Drum', for Linda Ronstadt and her Stone Poneys band. The song was a hit.

Later with The Monkees Nesmith continued his country experiments including an up-tempo country with a back-beat number, 'Papa Gene's Blues', on their first million-selling album, 'The Monkees' (Colgems). That song would have entered the record collections of millions of fans who'd normally cross the street to avoid a country song. He continued to place country songs on Monkees albums, culminating in the magnificent 'Listen To The Band' single in 1969. Having enjoyed mass exposure Nesmith left the teeny bop band to pursue his artistic interests in the marriage of country and rock.

Clearly ahead of his time, record companies failed to market the music properly but the records contained some classic cuts. Nesmith's first solo album, 'Magnetic South' (RCA), is still considered a masterpiece in country rock. But it wasn't just his own work that was important. Nesmith gave old friend Michael Martin Murphey a hand up the ladder by recording his 'What Am I Doin' Hangin' Round?' with The Monkees. The band also stumbled across a country-meets-folk song by John Stewart called 'Daydream Believer' and took it to number one. Stewart himself, spurred by the success and financial bonus, pursued a solo career and made some fine Californian country rock in the seventies. He made his finest album, 'California Bloodlines', in Nashville just as Bob Dylan was cutting his influential 'Nashville Skyline' album.

If Nesmith was a pioneer and catalyst right at the start, then Gram Parsons played a similar role a little later and with more commercial success. In the mid-sixties, The Byrds were America's Beatles. Their electrified folk-rock, complete with jangly guitars and plentiful harmonies, was riding high. They also had an ear for country and their 1968 album 'The Notorious Byrd Brothers' featured a handful of top country musicians. When The Byrds' Chris Hillman met up with Gram Parsons they discovered a mutual love for old-time country music, especially bluegrass, and after Parsons joined the band it was only a matter of time before he and Hillman pushed The Byrds in a country direction. Although many of his vocals were lost in the mix of the seminal 'Sweetheart Of The Rodeo', Parsons' influence and songs were crucial to the new direction the group were taking. When The Byrds were invited to perform on the *Grand Ole Opry* they performed Gram's 'Hickory Wind' to a somewhat subdued audience – in 1968 hippies and rednecks were diametrically opposed.

9

Parsons left The Byrds late in 1968 when he refused to tour South Africa, but the following year he was back with Hillman and a new band, The Flying Burrito Brothers, probably the finest country rock band of them all. Their début album 'Gilded Palace Of Sin' (A&M) sounded pretty country for a bunch of young long-haired rockers and its album sleeve typified the times with marijuana leaves embroidered into their Nudie suits. This was definitely a new kind of country music, certainly more Hank Williams than Jim Reeves. And if hip rock stars could like country music then maybe it wasn't parents' music after all.

The Burrito Brothers continued to make quality music but after their second album Parsons left for a solo career. In 1971 another Burrito, Bernie Leadon, left to form The Eagles. These artists may have been pioneers but if others hadn't followed there would have been no movement.

Fortunately several musicians were taken by the idea of combining country and rock. Rodney and Doug Dillard formed The Dillards in the late sixties and recorded for the fledgling Elektra Records. Their sound was deeply rooted in bluegrass but they spiced it up with rock arrangements and instrumentation. Their albums, 'Back Porch Bluegrass' and 'Live: Almost' were classics of their kind.

THE NEW RIDERS OF THE PURPLE SAGE

The New Riders Of The Purple Sage also gave rock fans a taste of country. Formed from The Grateful Dead (whose 'Workingman's Dead' album had a strong country feel) the early line-up featured Jerry Garcia on pedal steel guitar. Several musicians passed through the band over the years but by the mid-seventies their output had softened and become boring.

Commander Cody And The Lost Planet Airmen played a crazed country rock, Pure Prairie League went for a gentler harmony sound and Mike Nesmith put together (but was never a member of) Area Code 615, a talent heavy line-up, noted for Charlie McCoy's incredible harmonica playing.

Poco, a massive selling soft rock band in the late seventies, began a decade earlier as a credible country rock line-up. In 1968 Jim Messina and Richie Furey left Buffalo Springfield and recruited top steel player Rusty Young and Randy Meisner (later an Eagle) to form Poco who made several class albums before leaving their country roots later in the seventies.

The Eagles were easily the most successful country rock band of them all. Randy Meisner, Bernie Leadon, Glenn Frey and Don Henley sold millions of records with a harmony heavy, free-flowing country sound. Later they veered more in the direction of rock but their self titled début album remains a classic of country rock.

The music of these bands is clearly echoed in the contemporary sound of groups like Restless Heart, Highway 101 and The Desert Rose Band, but the West Coast country rock sound failed to have any real impact on Nashville at the time. It was the Texas rebels who forged lasting changes in the Nashville establishment, artists like Kris Kristofferson, Mickey Newbury, Willie Nelson and Waylon Jennings.

THE EAGLES, *LEFT TO RIGHT:* DON HENLEY, JOE WALSH, RANDY MEISNER, GLENN FREY AND DON FELDER

Kris Kristofferson played a key role in changing Nashville's attitudes towards country music artists. His scruffy, long-haired and bearded image was directly opposed to the clean-cut look that the country establishment demanded. His songs were honest, poetic, political and challenging; he talked about drugs. But such was his talent and charisma that Nashville was forced to follow his example rather than shut him out.

Kristofferson, a Texan, arrived in Nashville in 1965 and worked as a janitor for CBS but it wasn't until 1968 that Roger Miller covered his 'Me And Bobby McGee'. When Janis Joplin took the song to the top of the rock charts it was clear that Nashville had a star on its hands. Johnny Cash helped Kristofferson's acceptance by writing the sleeve notes for his self-titled début album (a role he repeated for Bob Dylan). He went on to score with a series of supremely personal, insightful and moving records before moving on to an acting career.

KRIS KRISTOFFERSON

They may be the elder statesmen of new country now but in the mid-seventies Willie Nelson and Waylon Jennings were both labelled 'outlaws'. Both singers took on Nashville and won. Tired of playing country music by numbers they sought artistic freedom and such was their talent and eventual selling power that they were able to write their own rules.

Nelson, from Waco, Texas, was a prolific songwriter in the late fifties and sixties, writing hits for artists such as Patsy Cline and Faron Young. But he became frustrated by the Nashville sound and tried to wriggle out of his RCA contract. Finally he succeeded and recorded two progressive albums for Atlantic, 'Shotgun Willie' and 'Phases And Stages'. Most importantly Nelson moved from Nashville to Austin, Texas, where he became the figurehead of a rebel country movement that included out-and-out rockers like Doug Sahm and sensitive writers like Guy Clark and Jerry Jeff Walker.

Like Nelson, Waylon Jennings became frustrated with record company restrictions. Even after years with RCA he was refused permission to choose his own band, songs and artistic direction. Finally, in the early seventies, he went over the heads of his Nashville bosses and struck a more satisfying deal with the New York office. His subsequent albums, 'Ladies Love Outlaws' and 'Honky Tonk Heroes' in 1973, proved that given freedom, Jennings was the perfect country rebel. The success of Nelson and Jennings caused Nashville to bend to their outlaw ways. The shackles loosened, at least for a while.

Other artists, notably Hank Williams Jr and Alabama, fused country with southern rock, adding a further dimension to country music, while Juice Newton continued similar interpretations into the mid-eighties. Crucially, all those acts sold vast quantities of records but with the move towards rock, and with West Coast country rock increasingly becoming bland after the mid-seventies, country music desperately needed a popular artist to maintain links with country roots. That artist was Emmylou Harris, still one of Nashville's finest performers and for a long period almost the lone voice of non-pop country in mainstream Nashville.

Late sixties Washington DC was a hotbed for acoustic music and Emmylou, stirred by the folk boom, entered the coffee houses armed with a case-load of songs and an acoustic guitar. She was spotted one night by Gram Parsons who invited her to work on 'GP' and 'Grievous Angel' (Warners). "Working with Gram was a wonderful experience," she says. "He was wildly misunderstood, too country for the rockers and too weird for the Nashville establishment. But he had a vision and a love for those old Louvins harmonies that was intense and powerful."

Parsons, a rich, mixed-up kid, was befriended by Keith Richards and his influence on The Rolling Stones can be heard on certain tracks on their first two seventies albums 'Sticky Fingers' and 'Exile On Main Street'. But the shadow of The Stones cast a dark cloud over Gram and he died a drug-related death in California on September 19 1973. The subsequent disappearance of his body and its discovery in a disinterred state at the Joshua Tree monument in the California desert is one of the more macabre episodes in rock folklore.

Emmylou was crushed but Gram's death inspired her. "I had no fire in me until Gram died. But afterwards I felt strongly that I had to continue his work. It was hard going solo but my attitude was always, 'How would Gram do this?' and somehow my sound evolved." From her début, 'Pieces Of The Sky' album to her 1988 effort 'Angel Band' (Warners) Harris has produced a series of impeccably tasteful, roots-dominated country and rock albums.

Even during the disco and pop obsessed late seventies Harris stood by her beliefs. "There was a time when country became very boring. Those were very frustrating times for those of us playing a rootsy acoustic style." At the height of country blandness, during the *Urban Cowboy* era that saw everyone and their dog regaling themselves in western gear and attempting to emulate the cool screen presence of John Travolta and Co, Emmylou Harris cut a pure country album, 'Roses In The Snow'. "It was the old-time sound, those Louvin harmonies, that first drew me to country music. And when I worked with Gram Parsons it was that feel that inspired us. So with 'Roses In The Snow' I was saying 'Take that you pop people'."

'Roses In The Snow' was a retrospective, nostalgic album. It recalled an era of innocence and honesty, the music was pure and uncluttered. The arranger was none other than Ricky Skaggs – later to turn traditional country into a million-dollar empire. Around the time of the release of 'Roses In The Snow', country music was entering a sales lull. The established artists on the major labels' rosters had peaked several years before. There was a block on new signings because established artists were still selling but not in the same quantities as before.

The fashion-based *Urban Cowboy* fad increased sales temporarily but once over, country was left in a depressed state. The artists were stale, the sound was stale and audiences and record buyers were in decline. Many record buyers had left country because of its bland pop colouring. If an artist could play top quality hard country, utilising modern studio techniques but maintaining a roots sound maybe those buyers would come back to country.

When Ricky Skaggs' first Epic album 'Waitin' For The Sun To Shine' went gold, the executives smiled. Maybe traditional country was the answer. History of course recognises that the old-time sound was the solution as Skaggs, Yoakam, The Judds, George Strait, Reba McEntire and a host of others proved through the eighties. A pool of talent was waiting to be tapped, a group of artists united by a common love of classic country. And as the doors opened to a new wave of talent, so a broad spectrum of country music made itself felt in eighties country music.

☆ ★ ★ ★ ☆

ABOVE:
EMMYLOU HARRIS
BELOW:
GRAM PARSONS

NEW COUNTRY/ A-Z

A

Terry Allen

Some artists seem destined to avoid commercial success while basking in an aura of cult acclaim. Born in Wichita, Kansas in 1943, Terry Allen is something of a country music renaissance man. An architect and art teacher as well as a performer and writer, his career since the early seventies has been peppered with outstanding concerts and recordings.

Everything he does has his own individual stamp – gruff vocals, incisive sometimes witty lyrics and a rolling piano style. For some time he's been part of the thriving Texas scene playing with, and working on albums by, the likes of Joe Ely, Butch Hancock and other Texas troubadours. His own albums have been rare jewels, and contain songs like 'New Delhi Freight Train' which was covered by Little Feat.

Back in 1975 Allen cut a concept album, 'Juarez' (Fate) about four people who migrate from California to Mexico, but it never sold in vast quantities and is not easy to find. Fortunately the album reached enough people and Allen achieved a cult notoriety, especially in Europe. His next, and finest album, 'Lubbock On Everything' (Fate) was first released in the US in 1978, and re-released last year in England by Special Delivery Records. It's a double album, filled with salty tales, Texan characters – the little people and the misfits, the good guys and the bad guys.

His albums since have been more diverse with 'Bloodlines' (Fate) the nearest to a classic Allen sound. In 1986 he worked with Talking Heads' David Byrne on the soundtrack for *True Stories* and performed 'Cocktail Desperado' – a song that only an irreverent, slightly off-the-wall thinker and writer like Allen could have created. Allen infuriates his many fans by sticking to a rigid, almost self-indulgent, desire to do as he wishes when he wishes. Such is the prerogative of multi-talented artists.

OPPOSITE:
BONO AND WYNONNA JUDD SINGING TOGETHER WHEN THE JUDDS JOINED U2 ON STAGE DURING THEIR 1987 JOSHUA TREE TOUR

15

John Anderson

Anderson's been in Nashville a while since trekking northwards from Florida in the early seventies. At first he struggled but those bluesy, raunchy vocals soon won him a deal with Warner Bros Records, though he now records for MCA. His album, 'The Best Of John Anderson' ('Greatest Hits' in the US) is one of the finest compilation albums in country music – no song is wasted, every tune a potential classic.

He crossed over into the American pop charts in 1983 with 'Swingin'' proving that, well before the new country movement opened its doors to a pioneer spirit, Anderson was doing his own thing. These days Anderson is re-discovering his writing talents. Last year he took time off the road and came up with his tenth studio album '10'. If Anderson continues in this vein, he'll maintain his position as one of Nashville's most exciting and adventurous artists.

Asleep At The Wheel

Asleep At The Wheel have become more of an institution than a band. Led by gentle giant Ray Benson for over 18 years, the band has employed around 75 different musicians over the years and Benson is the only original member remaining. Their début album 'Comin' Right At Ya' (United Artists) which was deleted but has been re-issued in Europe by Edsel, set a stylistic precedent – an earthy fusion of western swing, R&B, Cajun blues and contemporary rock – but the band has always dabbled and experimented. Benson refuses to pigeonhole the band's music, preferring to call it 'American Music'.

ASLEEP AT THE WHEEL, *LEFT TO RIGHT*: JOHN ELY, MIKE FRANCIS, DAVID SANGER, RAY BENSON, TIM ALEXANDER, JOHN MITCHELL AND LARRY FRANKLIN

Their latest album 'Western Standard Time' (Epic) sees Asleep At The Wheel down to a seven-piece, featuring (alongside Benson) Larry Franklin on fiddle, Tim Alexander on piano, John Ely on steel guitar, David Sanger on drums, John Mitchell on bass and Mike Francis on saxophone. The record opens with the old big band classic on which Benson duets with Willie Nelson, and elsewhere digs back into the roots of Texas music with tunes from Bob Wills and Ernest Tubb. Benson retains his enthusiasm for Asleep At The Wheel's heavy touring schedules (over 250 dates a year) by fostering outside interests, notably golf at which he regularly partners Willie Nelson and Huey Lewis.

Asleep At The Wheel have progressed from being a critics' band in the early seventies to a noted live act and are now part of the booming new traditionalist movement as they re-awaken the sounds of old-time Texas, albeit jazzed up in their own free form style.

Chris Austin

A new signing to Warner Bros, Chris Austin could possibly follow Ricky Skaggs' path from child prodigy to recording star. Austin grew up in Boone, North Carolina, a reserved kid who preferred the company of banjo, guitar, fiddle and mandolin to socialising and rough housing. At the age of 11 he was winning local talent and instrument contests. Chris attended college in West Texas but Nashville was too much of a lure and, as luck would have it, he stumbled across Ricky Skaggs backstage at the *Grand Ole Opry*. A quickly palmed demo tape became Austin's passport to a job in the Skaggs band. Now, with two years on the road under his belt, Austin is trying it out alone. Definitely a name to watch.

☆ ★ ★ ★ ☆

Baillie And The Boys

Unlike many of the new Nashville artists, this trio hail not from south of the Mason Dixon line but from Springsteen country, New Jersey. Kathie Baillie may be the obvious star of the show but husband Michael Bonagura and Alan LeBoeuf contribute a great deal with inspired harmonies and considerable writing skills. Michael and Alan first joined forces almost 20 years ago in a band called London Fog and met up with Kathie Baillie back in 1973. They hit it off musically and provided back-up vocals for a slew of important pop acts including Gladys Knight, The Ramones and Talking Heads. The band split temporarily in 1977 as Alan LeBoeuf spent two years playing Paul McCartney in the hit Broadway show, *Beatlemania*.

As the eighties turned however, the trio reformed and headed for Nashville to sing back-up for veteran star Ed Bruce. Their talents quickly spread around the Nashville grapevine and all three were signed as writers to Picalic Music. Not long afterwards RCA Records signed the trio after a half-hour live audition in their offices. "That blend of three-part harmony, strong musicianship and impressive writing skills make Baillie And The Boys one of the most promising young acts," says Joe Galante, RCA's Nashville President. The début album, 'Baillie And The Boys' (RCA) is produced by two of Nashville's finest knob twiddlers, Paul Davis and Kyle Lehning. After 15 years in the business Baillie And The Boys are all set for overnight success.

Pinto Bennett

Sometimes it takes a trip abroad for an American country artist to be appreciated in their own country. Boxcar Willie didn't achieve fame until he'd won over audiences in England. A similar fate could soon befall Idaho honky tonker Pinto Bennett. Bennett is no spring chicken and the image is more outlaw than George Strait but his music, writing and band, The Famous Motel Cowboys, are of the highest order.

Raised on an Idaho ranch, Bennett grew up listening to old-time country. "I loved Lefty (Frizell) and Hank Williams," he remembers. During the sixties Bennett fused his honky tonk style with the burgeoning country rock styles and throughout the seventies made money from gigging. In 1982 Bennett gave Nashville a shot but ended up digging ditches rather than winning a spot on the Opry.

Disillusioned but heartened by advice picked up from fellow artist and ditch digger Richard Dobson, Bennett went home, cut an album and sailed it across to England. A new country label, PT Records picked it up and Bennett is poised for success with an outstanding third album, 'Pure Quill' of roadhouse country rock. In an era of nine-to-five musicians Bennett is a throwback to those who lived and breathed for their music.

Larry Boone

If the clean-cut, all-American approach of George Strait and Randy Travis is a guarantee of success then Larry Boone should soon follow those two as a country music superstar. An outstanding athlete at college and no fool in the class room, Boone opted for a career in music rather than on the sports field or behind a word processor (he fancied a career as a sportswriter for a while).

Boone writes and sings old-time country. His voice is warm, mellow and pure and his writing talents have already provided songs for Lacy J. Dalton, Ed Bruce, Michael Martin Murphey, Don Williams and Marie Osmond. Boone headed for Nashville in 1980, before the doors were properly opened for the new traditional sound. He played at the Wax Museum, a Nashville tourist attraction, for tips for a while before bumping into Gene Ferguson, a former vice president of CBS who had recently left the corporation to concentrate on managing John Anderson and Charly McClain.

Boone won a development deal with CBS but remembers that . . . "At that time they were puttin' out those records that were soft soundin' rock. My sound is country. I can't do anything about that." While the solo career failed to materialise Boone concentrated on honing his stage craft – "I guess I learned how to entertain during those years" – and paid the rent with several of his songs recorded by other artists.

Times were changing in the mid-eighties: George Strait was a superstar playing stone country and Randy Travis was taking off. Some have accused Boone of following in their wake, in fact his style dates back before Travis' amazing success, but Boone had to wait for his break. It came in 1986 when the enigmatic Steve Popovich signed Boone to Polygram. The self-titled début album, produced by Ray Baker who produced early George Strait, Merle Haggard and Moe Bandy shows that Boone could soon rival both Strait and Travis as the Kingpin of old time swinging, smooth honky tonk.

Boone has paid his dues. In 1988 he toured extensively picking up a large body of support. He's happy with the album that recalls Haggard and George Jones with a slight hint of those veritable blues stylists Ray Charles and BB King. Like the best in country music Boone manages to sing sad, sentimental material without sounding insincere or maudlin. Writing is important to him. "Songs have to evoke the right emotions," he believes. "It's important to find the right words and not quit until you have them." Boone's vocal talents, perfectionism, good looks and easy going but charismatic stage presence mark him out as a dynamic new prospect. The début album will not be his last.

T. Graham Brown

Country music has always been a broad church. In Texas German settlers introduced a polka beat, in the Appalachians Irish and Scottish folk songs turned into Virginia reels, in Louisiana the French threw up a Cajun brew and in Memphis a steamy mix of blues and soul grew up not far down the road from Nashville. Many country artists have dabbled with blues and soul but very few have achieved such polished results as one of the nicest men in the business, T. Graham Brown.

Brown is a beaming effervescent character who's as enthusiastic about his music now as he was nearly 15 years ago when it all started at the University of Georgia. He and a friend played rock pop and beach music at the Athens Holiday Inn. "We made good money in those days," he remembers, "and I guess that's when I decided that music should be my career. I kinda got interested in that whole outlaw scene and lived through what I call my 'David Allan Coe period' . . . you know, long hair, black cowboy hat and the whole boogie."

After an excursion into outlaw country Brown went back to soulful blues and rock. "We played black music mainly, though we'd throw in some John Fogerty tunes and Van Morrison's 'Brown Eyed Girl' occasionally." remembers His 'T'ness as he's fondly known. In 1982 Brown headed for Nashville. He struggled for a long time and pays a great debt to his wife for those early days. "I couldn't have done it without her. She worked and supported me while I knocked on doors and worked on my songs. I'll never forget what she did for me." It may not have been what he wanted but Brown won some plum jobs singing demos and doing jingles for, among others, Kraft, McDonalds and Coca Cola. "I was getting a lot of work from publishers doing demos and that helped to get my voice known," he recalls.

Not long after Capitol/EMI America hired Terry Choate as head of A&R, and luckily for Brown, Choate, already a fan, quickly signed the big-voiced singer. His first single hit 39 in the country charts and after that it was top 10s all the way. With country music booming in Europe, EMI selected Brown to play some showcases in Europe. He won over international EMI representatives, all of Europe wanted a T. Graham Brown packaging deal. Brown's début album, 'I Tell It Like It Used To Be' (Capitol) gave him two number ones and two top 10 singles. Not a bad start for an artist stylistically on the edge of Nashville country music.

But T. Graham Brown had several factors in his favour: vocally he's head and shoulders above many country crooners. His music mixes the best in southern styles – a little bit Elvis, a little bit Otis Redding. His prime advantage over other talented hopefuls however is his endearing stage persona. When the lights go down and the band hit those opening bars and Brown recalls a four-year-old in front of a Christmas tree, his enthusiasm and sheer love of the music is uplifting and infectious. He may not be pure country but Nashville has taken him to its heart. And even as the follow-up albums to 'I Tell It Like It Used To Be', 'Brilliant Conversationalist' (Capitol) and 'Come As You Were' (Capitol), continue down the road of country soul and blues, when he plays a country tune, notably Harlan Howard's 'She's Okay And I'm Okay' from his latest LP 'Come As You Were' (Capitol), it's very clear that His 'T'Ness is still a country boy at heart.

"I don't care what they call it, blues or rock or R&B or soul as long as they don't forget that it's country blues or country soul or country R&B. I'm proud to be a country singer and while I may throw in other styles the country part of it is the most important to me."

The Burch Sisters

Newly signed to the Mercury label, this energetic trio, the three Cs, Cathy, Charlene and Cindy, sing like nightingales and perform with heartfelt fizz and passion. Female vocal acts may be in vogue but this trio stands no chance of being lost in the crowd. Less traditional than some of their Nashville cohorts, Burch music is gospel and pop tinged but the cascading three-voice harmonies are pure country.

Based in Screven, a small town in Georgia, the sisters started taking their music seriously in the mid-eighties and won a state talent contest in 1986. They saved their money (Cathy works as a horse trainer, Charlene's a nurse and Cindy a radiologist) and recorded a demo in Atlanta. The tapes finally made their way to Polygram Senior Vice President Steve Popovich and the act joined the Mercury roster.

☆ ★ ★ ★ ☆

Mary Chapin Carpenter

Singer songwriter Carpenter is slightly more folk than country perhaps, but her music is literate, personal and beautifully melodic. A new signing to CBS, her début album, 'Hometown Girl' (CBS) proves that she's an artist in the Nanci Griffith, Guy Clark mould.

Mary Chapin (a double moniker like Mary Beth or Mary Jane) was born in Princeton – "a small town in New Jersey with lots of pretty houses." She first learned guitar at school and later moved to Washington DC. Mary thrived on the booming acoustic music scene in Washington and was soon performing in clubs and bars. She writes from experience, a throwback to the introspective singer songwriters of the

seventies. Along with her guitar player and producer John Jennings, Carpenter released an independent label album.

In 1986 she won a collection of awards at the Washington Area Music Awards. The publicity put her on bills with performers like John Hiatt and Kris Kristofferson. Eventually a tape found its way to CBS and the result was 'Hometown Girl', a songwriter's album that reaches into the heart of the listener with a rare beauty and power.

Rosanne Cash

Rosanne Cash plays country with a rock 'n' roll attitude. The daughter of Johnny Cash and his first wife Vivian Liberto, she was the first hip country star of the eighties. She spoke out about the drugs problem, performed with a sexual swagger and wrote songs with challenging and insightful lyrics. As a parent she has battled to do things her own way and organize her life around her family. Rosanne Cash is uncompromising and forward thinking and it's likely to be easier for women to make a mark in country music thanks to her example.

She was born in Memphis in 1955 just as her father was tasting the seeds of success, but grew up in Southern California. From a young age she saw the problems of success and the results of bigotry. "We had TV cameras in our house. We all hated it especially my mother who was a shy person. She was Italian and I remember the Ku Klux Klan burned a cross on our front yard because he (Johnny Cash) spoke out in favour of Indian rights." After high school graduation Rosanne and her step-sister Rosey joined the Cash show, first as laundry workers, later as back-up singers. "My father said to me, 'Here's a list of 100 essential country songs – you have to know them if you want to be my daughter'," she remembers.

But Rosanne was still working things out. She witnessed first hand the traumas of celebrity life, regarding Nashville as a backwater and still undecided over what she wanted for herself. She took acting classes in New York and even worked in the CBS

Records' London office for a year in the mid-seventies. She enrolled in a writing and acting class at Nashville's Vanderbilt University but she still had to come to terms with her music. When Ariola Records in Germany expressed an interest she went along for the ride and although she wasn't too keen on the resultant album she spent much of her time writing to the man who'd produced her demos, Texan musician Rodney Crowell. They have been together ever since. Fortunately for the still nervous Rosanne, Ariola only released that début album in Germany and CBS offered her the chance to record a fresh set with Crowell as producer.

'Right Or Wrong', her début album, received great critical acclaim with its rocky country sound due largely to Rodney Crowell's fine band The Cherry Bombs.

The next album, 'Seven Year Ache' continued the progressive style and contained two number ones and a Grammy nomination. The third album, 'Somewhere In The Stars' came out in 1982 and featured a collaboration with Crowell, 'Looking For A Corner'. Significantly, in the light of her innovative new video company, this album spawned a video for 'I Wonder' produced by Michael Nesmith (former Monkee and excellent early seventies country artist) and was nominated for an American Video Award.

Rosanne Cash's output has hardly been prolific. Her values don't place promotion and touring above her personal life. But there is no questioning the quality. Her two recent albums, 'Rhythm And Romance' and 'King's Record Shop', have continued the rock meets country feel and proved that Rosanne is a songwriter par excellence (she won a 1987 BMI writing award.) Musically she's been a pioneer right through the eighties and it wasn't until very recently that the likes of Steve Earle were able to follow her lead. Moreover she proved that artistic integrity could survive in Nashville and concentrated on singing and performing songs that dealt with more than simple heartbreak.

"Most country songs go something like, 'Oh honey you left me and now I'm sad', but I'm more interested in the hidden agenda, 'Oh honey you left me and why did I want you to do that'," she states. One song on 'Kings Record Shop', 'Rosie Strike Back', a perfect example of her progressive, eighties voice, encourages a woman who suffers physical abuse to stand up for herself and refuse to take it. A far cry from 'Stand By Your Man'.

But even that is only the tip of the iceberg, "How far does one go in speaking out against abuse," she asks. "Does it mean for a woman not hiding your intellectual abilities, or not playing the weak part just to make some guy feel better? There are so many subtle levels and a lot of them are a kind of self-imposed victimization. And those things are definitely rampant in the culture – all the way back to when women were considered property."

After all these years Rosanne Cash understands that her work has worth. "I don't much care about being a celebrity, but I do care about being an artist."

Guy Clark

Ask any of the new breed of Nashville songwriters – Lyle Lovett, Darden Smith, Steve Earle, Nanci Griffith – who was their major modern-day influence and the chances are that the name of Guy Clark will come up five times out of six. Clark has been on the scene in Texas and Nashville for around 20 years and has never enjoyed the commercial success his talent would suggest. But as a writer he still produces material for all the new country types and is one of the most respected song craftsmen in Music City.

"I'm from Texas, West Texas. When I was a kid I lived in a hotel in a little place called Mochas," – the setting for many of his finest songs, 'Desperadoes Waiting For A Train' for example. Clark headed for Houston in the sixties hanging out and playing with Jerry Jeff Walker and Townes Van Zandt. "I played folk music," he recalls. "Until I started writing around 1966 and then my own kind of country and blues style just happened."

After a stint in Los Angeles Clark headed east for Nashville but the town wasn't ready for his dusty-voiced ballads and country boogie. Sticking around he finally made an album for RCA, 'Old No 1' that is still regarded as one of the finest albums of all time. "I'm real proud of that record although it sounds like we could have spent some more time technically when I listen to it now," says Clark. The album and its almost as impressive follow-up 'Texas Cooking' (RCA) spawned a number of cover versions. Both were deleted but have been re-issued by Edsel in Europe. Jerry Jeff Walker and David Allen Coe had hits with 'Desperadoes' and Johnny Cash growled through Clark's 'The Last Gunfighter Ballad'.

Lack of commercial success disappoints Clark but he's quick to realise that unlike many other artistically minded writers he does make a living from his songs. "You know it'd be nice to have hits myself but I don't think my singing really appeals to country radio." Clark parted company with RCA in 1977 and joined Warners for the self-titled 1977 album, but while the songs maintained a poetic integrity, they failed to set the record shops alight.

These days Clark sees himself as a performer in demand and a well respected songwriter. He takes his craft seriously. "I'm a perfectionist with my songs often spending too long on them and that can be a real danger because you can break the spirit of the song," he says. His wife Susannah has been with him throughout his recording career, co-writing and singing harmony but these days she's a busy visual artist in Nashville. Guy Clark is not bitter about his ability to avoid commercial success. He's something of a father-figure to the new breed. "Back in Texas I can remember trying to persuade Steve Earle to use a lighter gauge of string – he would strum so hard." He played a major part in Lyle Lovett coming to the attention of A&R man Tony Brown at MCA. But with a more open-minded climate prevailing in Nashville, Clark could still be a star, even as a veteran.

Earl Thomas Conley

Country music has always enjoyed a solid bedrock of support in America's blue collar land, and Earl Thomas Conley captures this spirit with a rare articulateness and gift for melody. The gruff-voiced singer has flowered in recent years but he has been knocking on music business doors for over 10 years. Born in Ohio, he developed a liking for the music he heard on the radio – Hank Williams, Jimmy Martin and Bill Monroe – but it was the excitement of rock 'n' roll that drew him to making music his career.

In the late sixties Conley trekked to Nashville every few months in an effort to create interest in his work. In 1970 he plucked up courage and moved to Music City and within months Conway Twitty took his 'This Time I've Hurt Her More' to the number one spot. Conley cut an album for the small Sunbird label, 'Blue Pearl', and he enjoyed his first solo number one single with 'Fire And Smoke'. RCA recognised his potential and released an album also entitled 'Fire And Smoke' in 1980.

Conley's style was set. His vocals are gruff, the songs poetic and colourful. Eschewing glitz and image Conley recalls early Kristofferson and to his credit he has continued to progress and move with the times. His second RCA album, 'Somewhere Between Right And Wrong' was a shade more contemporary than his début effort,

while his third, 'Don't Make It Easy For Me' spawned a slew of chart-topping singles. His career has progressed more quietly than some Nashville stars but there's no doubting Conley's quality.

While others may come and go Conley has proved his ability to maintain an artistic integrity while continuing to move with the times. His 1988 album, 'The Heart Of It All' fits neatly between mainstream and new country. Conley works hard and quietly, but his importance to Nashville has not gone unnoticed.

Rodney Crowell

Crowell is one of the most influential of Nashville's newer set of writers, artists and producers. Throughout the eighties his production work for his wife Rosanne Cash has won him an enviable reputation, his songs have been recorded by numerous mainstream artists and his own status as a performer and recording star have seen him move from well respected industry man to commercially successful country and rock artist with his excellent 1988 'Diamonds And Dirt' album (CBS).

Born and raised in Houston, Texas, Crowell could hardly avoid music. His grandfather played bluegrass banjo, his grandmother guitar and his father played as a sideman in numerous bars and honky tonks. Initially Rodney took up drums but later became an innovative and accomplished guitarist. In the early days Crowell played in rock bands. "I was such a fan of The Beatles and Presley and Dylan, I mean I still am but in those days that was the kind of music I wanted to play." As country rock made country acceptable and progressive, Crowell re-examined his Texas roots and began to turn towards country music.

In the early seventies he moved to Nashville determined to make it as a writer. He impressed Jerry Reed who took him on as a songwriter and Crowell won himself a reputation around Nashville. Guy Clark took him under his wing and a meeting with Emmylou Harris's manager, Brian Ahern, led to him moving to California to join Emmylou's Hot Band. His writing abilities impressed Emmylou and she recorded many of his songs including 'Amarillo', 'Till I Gain Control', 'Tulsa Queen' and 'I Ain't Livin' Long Like This'.

He embarked on a solo career in 1977 recording for Warner Bros and his début album, 'I Ain't Livin' Long Like This', was released in 1978. The seed of his current style, contemporary country that is sparse and tough but full of musical twists and lyrical turns, was sown on that album. "I've never been a straight country singer but I

do play real country songs as well as all out rock material. I mean to me country and rock 'n' roll are much the same. You listen to Hank Williams and Carl Perkins or Chuck Berry and there's not too much difference."

Crowell's advantage over the past decade is that he's always kept an open mind about music. He's more likely to listen to John Lennon or Elvis Costello albums than standard Nashville output. Consequently when he cuts a country album a whole range of influences and styles are fused together within a country format. Crowell recorded two more albums for Warners, 'What Will The Neighbours Think?' and 'Rodney Crowell' and at the same time became involved with Rosanne Cash as her husband, writing partner and producer. Being married to a star wasn't easy for Crowell and he and Rosanne's life was peppered with trauma, not least a burgeoning drugs problem. "The problem with drugs is that people begin to lean on them for inspiration and that never works."

A deal with CBS helped put his life in order. The first CBS album, 'Street Language' co-produced with old friend and band member Tony Brown, saw Crowell relaxed and musically adventurous. His 1988 album, 'Diamonds And Dirt' is his most country album to date and also his most successful. "Tony Brown persuaded me to slack off trying to be an artist all the time and just do some good country songs. The writing came together, we kept the sound sparse and it's been liked by country radio. I'm real pleased."

These days Crowell has an office on Music Row in Nashville and is enthusiastic about the current health of Nashville. "The town is opening up and people like Tony Brown are gaining positions of power so yeah, I'm optimistic that country will continue to rediscover that kind of cutting edge which it lost for a while back there."

☆ ★ ★ ★ ☆

The Desert Rose Band

Hailed by one critic as, 'The most brilliant new country act of 1987' the Desert Rose Band has taken Nashville by storm. The group may be a new unit but the principals are country and rock veterans. Lead singer and chief songwriter is Chris Hillman, bass player and founding member of one of America's finest bands, The Byrds. It is 20 years since The Byrds' seminal 'Sweetheart Of The Rodeo' (CBS) album changed the face of country and rock. And now Hillman is back at the fore of progressive country having pioneered country rock with The Flying Burrito Brothers, Manassas and several outstanding solo projects.

With a pedigree like that it is hardly surprising that the band leader has surrounded himself with great players. Herb Pederson has been an outstanding session man for many years and his harmony work on the two Desert Rose Band albums, 'Desert Rose Band' (Curb/MCA) and 'Running' (Curb/MCA) is outstanding. John Jorgenson contributes guitar and mandolin, steel guitar wizard Jay Dee Maness brings his own West Coast style, and the rhythm section is Bill Bryson on bass and Steve Duncan on drums.

Hillman's Californian upbringing opened his eyes to the likes of Buck Owens, Wynn Stewart, Rose Maddox – country artists with a subtle difference. "There were different influences in the music in California that you didn't have in Tennessee – like Mexican music," he says.

DESERT ROSE BAND, *LEFT TO RIGHT:* BILL BRYSON, JAY DEE MANESS, JOHN JORGENSON, CHRIS HILLMAN, HERB PEDERSEN AND STEVE DUNCAN

Hillman and Pederson played up-tempo bluegrass together as teenagers. In the mid-sixties Hillman joined The Byrds and in 1968 teamed up with Gram Parsons to push the group away from folk rock and into country rock. Rock music fans found it too country and country fans weren't ready for the free-form flowing country rock sound, and The Byrds received a very flat reception at a *Grand Ole Opry* guest spot. Undeterred Hillman and Parsons continued their pioneering work with The Flying Burrito Brothers, one of the finest country rock bands of the early seventies.

A mid-seventies Byrds reunion fell flat. "We didn't know what we were doing or who we were any more," Hillman recalls. We opted to break up as friends. I wanted to get away from the business and I went back to playing acoustic, me and Al Perkins." His enthusiasm renewed, Hillman cut a couple of solo albums for Sugar Hill, 'Morning Sky' and 'Desert Rose'. The beginnings of his current work can be found in these, especially the latter.

The Desert Rose Band came together in 1985. "Herb, John, Bill and I opened for Dan Fogelberg when he was doing a solo tour, playing bluegrass acoustically. I had a lot of songs and didn't want them done acoustically. We added Jay Dee Maness and Steve and literally played anywhere we could around LA," explains Hillman.

A batch of excellent songs, coupled with the band's experience and talent led to immediate success. Their first album had four hit singles and 'Running' further exhibits their easy fusion of country and rock 'n' roll. Says Hillman, "The Desert Rose Band to me is a highly tuned, highly evolved version of what I was doing 20 years ago. I just feel we're doing it better now. I guess you could call it country-rock or West Californian country music . . . "

Dean Dillon

Best known until now as a songwriter for George Strait, Dillon is set to become a star in his own right. From Lake City, Tennessee, Dillon was a spirited teenager. He left home at 17 fired by music, and hit Nashville at the tender age of 18. "I was just a long-haired boy from East Tennessee," recalls Dillon. He won a spot on a show at the Opryland theme park and eventually signed to Pi-Gem as a writer who drew on his own life experiences (and at an early age he'd had a few) and by 25 he was one of the hottest writers in town.

His abilities led to a contract with RCA and he later teamed up with Gary Stewart but only achieved minor success. "The problem was," Dillon believes, "that we were portrayed as outlaws, that I was crazy. I was real misunderstood for a long time in this town." Fortunately for Dillon his songwriting for George Strait resulted in a string of excellent recordings, 'Marina Del Ray', 'The Chair', 'Famous Last Words Of A Fool' and 'Ocean Front Property' among others.

In the last couple of years Dillon has matured and Capitol gave him another chance to bid for solo stardom. The début album for Capitol, 'Slick Nickel', saw him teamed with producer Randy Scraggs and a host of top-notch players – Johnny Gimble, Jerry Douglas, Vince Gill, Don Potter and others. The album ripples with life, a new traditionalist sound laced with heartfelt singing and tough but melodic material.

Richard Dobson

Richard Dobson is a poet, a musical visionary whose songs are timeless vignettes, everyday tales of everyday folk. So far fame has eluded this Texan giant but like Guy Clark he refuses to forgo his artistic principles in the search for money and glory.

These days his fan club includes John Prine, Steve Earle and Nanci Griffith whose plugging of her hero in concert has done the man's career no harm at all.

Dobson hails from Texas but he travelled extensively, learning to play guitar in South America. Faced by the draft in the sixties, Dobson enrolled at the University Of St Thomas, Houston and joined the Peace Corps. He served a musical apprenticeship in Texas folk clubs alongside Guy Clark and Townes Van Zandt, then it was off to Nashville but few of his songs, save a David Allan Coe cut of 'Piece Of Wood And Steel', were being recorded. He quit Nashville for the Texas Gulf Coast and released an album, 'In Texas Last December'. From that point he picked up a larger following culminating with a cover of 'Baby Ride Easy' by Dave Edmunds and Carlene Carter which persuaded him to give Nashville another shot.

He's still there, still a cult act and writer and still making records. His latest, 'State Of The Heart', is a live album and deserves more than mail order promotion. Nanci Griffith calls him 'The Hemingway Of Country Music' and it's almost a crime that more people haven't discovered the sensitivity and poetry of Richard Dobson.

Holly Dunn

Holly Dunn really was an overnight success. She appeared from nowhere to record a self-titled album for the fledgling MTM label in 1986 and the following year won the prestigious Horizon Award from the Country Music Association. She's currently riding high as one of the vanguard of women artists in Nashville.

From San Antonio, Texas, Holly learned guitar while a young girl and became lead singer with the Freedom Folk Singers and wound up representing Texas at the White House Bicentennial celebrations in 1976. At University she was a member of the Hilltop Singers but she hankered after a country music career. Coming to Nashville she sang lead and harmony on hundreds of demo tapes and finally signed as a full-time writer for CBS songs.

In 1987 she signed for MTM and soon had a massive hit with the Grammy award-nominated, 'Daddy's Hands' from her self-titled début album. She was also named the Academy Of Country Music's top new female artist in 1987 and won the Country Music Association's similar Horizon Award the same year.

Her second album, 'Cornerstone' (MTM) included contributions from top new talent Mark O'Connor and Bill Lloyd. It was her third effort, 'Across The Rio Grande', that pushed her to stardom. Holly shared the production chores and recruited top-flight musicians – Vince Gill, Jerry Douglas, Sam Bush – and came up with a punchy, varied but still cohesive traditional-sounding country album.

☆　★　★　★　☆

Steve Earle

Earle's 1986 album for MCA, 'Guitar Town' captured the imagination of the new country audience. Closer to Bruce Springsteen than Glen Campbell, Earle's style was fast, guitar dominated and laden with heavy southern drumming. The songs came from the heart, impassioned pleas from a blue collar wasteland and some of the most graceful ballads Nashville has ever cut. While Dwight Yoakam grabbed the kids' attention with the recreation of a style they never knew, Earle strapped on his six-string and rocked his heart out. He's probably the most progressive of all Nashville's new buckaroos and his 1988 album, 'Copperhead Road' (MCA) veers ever closer to a mainstream rock sound.

Steve Earle moved to Nashville from Texas in 1974, teaming up with other folky singer songwriters, Guy Clark, Townes Van Zandt and Rodney Crowell. "I guess I was playing folk music rather than mainstream country. When I was a kid it was really uncool to like country so I let it slip by, but with Waylon and Willie and the whole outlaw thing I felt comfortable coming back to that kind of music," says Earle.

For several years Earle struggled with little success. He signed a few publishing deals but . . . "I never made more than a thousand dollars a year until I was 30-years-old. Those companies like to keep you hungry until you get a hit record." A move back to Texas resulted in Earle forming a back-up band and they went on the road as Steve Earle And The Dukes. Back in Nashville he could cut full-sounding demos and in 1983 Epic offered the chunky Texan a recording contract. It didn't work out. "They saw me as a rockabilly act," he remembers. "And while I liked to play that kind of music, I felt trapped."

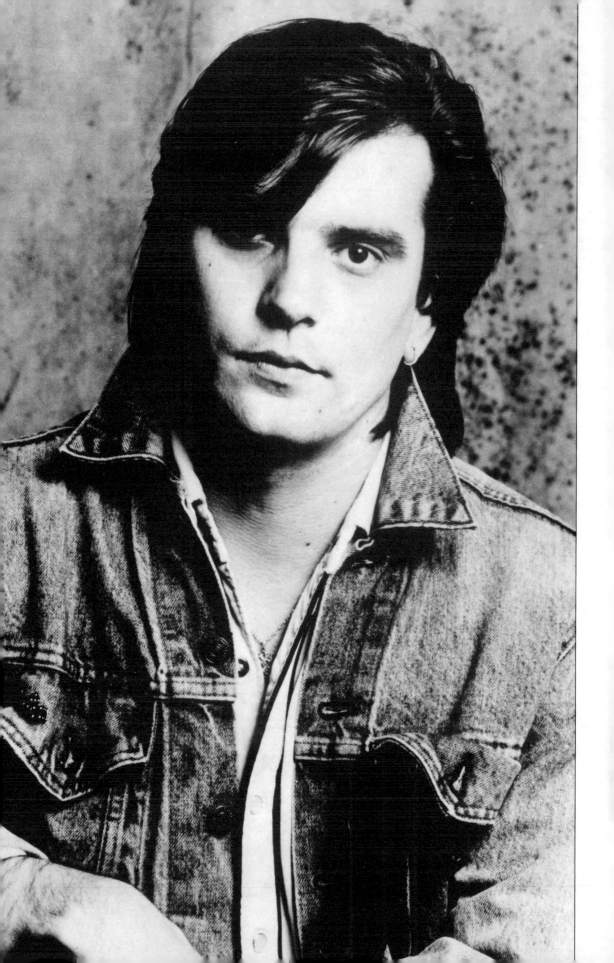

Meantime Tony Brown was taking up a senior position in A&R at MCA Records. A friend of Earle's, he listened to some of Steve's material, including 'Guitar Town'. "When I heard that song," says Brown, "I said, 'Hell that's great. Aren't CBS interested?' and he said they'd heard it but didn't like it. I knew it was good and had a feeling that Earle's style could break a few barriers."

Fortune smiled and Earle was signed by Tony Brown. The album (produced by Brown himself) caused a stir in Nashville. It sounded rock but there was no doubting Earle's country inflections and country topics. He couldn't understand the labelling problems.

"To me," says Earle, "good country and good rock 'n' roll have always been the same. They have never been mutually exclusive. They both have good lyrics, they tell the truth and have a passion you can't mistake for anything else." Earle likes to talk; barely pausing for breath he'll espouse opinions on Reagan's America (he's no fan of the Washington movie star), cars (he likes them fast), women (he's been married four times) and music. As a writer he captures the mood of small-town America notably on the punchy 'Someday' from the début MCA album in which a filling station attendant dreams of leaving his confines 'someday'.

Earle won immediate acclaim in Europe and became a favourite of the rock press in America. *Rolling Stone* named him top country artist and he received glowing write-ups in *The New York Times* and *Newsweek*. The follow-up album, 'Exit O' continued the trend away from straight country arrangements. The band play as one and Earle's lyrics always bite. The stand out track, 'The Rain Came Down', written especially for the *Farm Aid* concert, is a perfect example of Earle's ability to tackle political issues from a localised, human point of view.

Earle is ambitious. "I want to be up there with U2 not competing with Dan Seals," he says and his third MCA album, 'Copperhead Road' moves closer to Springsteen or John Cougar Mellencamp territory. But that's not to say his country leanings have been forgotten. There's a breezy bluegrass treatment on one tune and vocally he still sounds like a country boy. The failure of country radio to take Earle to its heart sees his affairs being moved out of Nashville to New York. Whether Earle will break into the mainstream rock world remains to be seen.

Joe Ely

Of all the seventies Texas songwriters and performers, Joe Ely has become the most visible. At his commercial peak in the early eighties he toured with UK punk band The Clash, a clue that his brand of country is tough, gritty and hard-edged.

Raised in Lubbock just down the road from Buddy Holly's old house, Ely quit school early for the bars and clubs. He teamed up with a bunch of friends including Butch Hancock and Jimmie Gilmore and they formed an acoustic country band called The Flatlanders who won great critical acclaim in Europe years after the band had broken up. Their only LP is now available in Europe through Charley Records.

After touring Ely resumed playing with an electric band in Lubbock and record companies began to take notice. MCA put up the cash for a début self-titled album and two follow ups, 'Honky Tonk Masquerade' and 'Down On The Drag', but commercial success eluded him. Long before the new country movement of the eighties Ely was mixing electric rock with Texas country but in hindsight his sound was ahead of its time.

Recently Ely has signed for Hightone Records (the label that launched Robert Cray) and his albums are released with great interest by Demon Records in the UK where Ely has a loyal and devoted following. His 1987 album, 'Lord Of The Highway' (Hightone) was a dark and brooding affair and his 1988 offering 'Dig All Night' (Hightone) featured David Grissom on guitar and roared with a hungry country energy.

Skip Ewing

Newly signed to MCA Records, Skip Ewing looks set to follow in the steps of label mates George Strait and Reba McEntire in putting a fresh and dynamic voice to a traditional sound. Born into a military family, Ewing travelled extensively as a kid but always found time to tune in to the nearest country station. His father bought him a guitar at the tender age of four and the young Skip soon fell in love with the music of Merle Haggard. "That was it, I was hooked," he says. "I knew that's what I wanted to do. I wanted to be able to get up there and sing and tear somebody's heart out and say something that really means something, because that's what Haggard did for me."

By the time he was ready for Nashville, Ewing was a competent musician and a budding songwriter. It took him a year-and-a-half to have his first song recorded and then the gates opened and George Jones, George Strait and Charley Pride were after his songs. Jimmy Bowen was eager to sign Ewing to MCA, even cutting short a vacation to finish the deal. Contract negotiations, usually long-winded affairs, were rushed through. Bowen encouraged Ewing to play a full part in the production of his first album, 'The Coast Of Colorado'. The record is proof that Skip Ewing has what it takes to play and sing traditional country music which for a man in his early twenties is no mean feat.

☆ ★ ★ ★ ☆

Rosie Flores

Like Dwight Yoakam, Rosie Flores plays a West Coast rock-influenced country music. Unlike many female artists she's a mean guitar player who struts across stages like Janis Joplin's hillbilly cousin. Born in San Antonio Texas, Rosie's earliest influences included Mexican and Tex Mex music, as well as Buck Owens and Elvis. At 12 her family moved north to San Diego, California, where she first took music seriously with an all-girl country-meets-rock-meets-psychedelia band called Penelope's Children.

Having learned her craft, Flores eventually felt comfortable enough to go out as a solo act performing original material before picking up an all-male back-up band, The Screamers, who made quite a stir in post-punk LA. The band broke up but Rosie

continued to play opening shows for David Lindley, Bo Diddley, Joe Ely and others. She again opted for a band, this time the all-girl The Screamin' Sirens who were well received in Los Angeles and even appeared in a movie *The Running Kind*. But Rosie was getting more involved in country music and in 1985 put together a four-track demo which won her a deal with Warner Bros.

Working with Dwight Yoakam as producer on the album, Rosie Flores quickly impressed those around her. Her singing style is raunchy but powerful while her guitar playing is innovative and gives the stage show a lift. Rosie Flores' music is definitely rooted in Californian country and the rock tinge has won her a young audience. How she progresses is largely down to her. She has the talent to produce pure country or to tackle a rock career. In the meantime the self-titled début album is sure to convert a number of rock fans to the country cause.

The Forester Sisters

They may have come along in the wake of The Judds, all glossy vocals and mountain harmonies, but in the four years they've been recording The Forester Sisters have forged their own identity as highly professional, impeccably turned out performers with more than a few roots in old-time country. Not as traditional as some of Nashville's newer acts, they still sing like mountain people even if the material is contemporary and perfect for a pop crossover.

The four sisters have been singing together most of their lives. From Lookout Mountain, Georgia (the last hideout of the Cherokee Indians on the Trail Of Tears), the sisters have that natural harmony sound only found in brother or sister combinations.

Kathy, Kim, Christy and June began singing in church and played in various groups and bands before deciding to go it alone as a sisters act. Christy, the youngest, joined full-time in 1982 and the quartet were approached by Warner Bros in 1984. Kathy Forester still finds it hard to believe. "Everything happened so fast. We did a showcase for the executives at Warners and they offered to sign us that night. It seems like we haven't stopped since."

The first self-titled album made quite a mark in country music, yielding three chart-topping singles (a record for a début album) and they found themselves sharing concert bills with Ricky Skaggs, Alabama, Merle Haggard and many other country legends. Their up-front personalities and *Dynasty* good looks made them darlings of the chat show circuit but Kathy is still adamant that the music comes before image. "We are singers first and foremost. Obviously we want to look good but without the songs there'd be nothing."

The second album, 'Perfume, Ribbons and Pearls' consolidated their success and touring took up more and more of their time. "It's kinda hard to have a personal life when you're on the road so much but we manage and wouldn't trade it for anything," says Kathy. The third and fourth albums, 'You Again' and 'Sincerely' saw the women singing even better, choosing material that suits them and creating a sound that's contemporary without being pop, and old-time without the hillbilly.

Foster And Lloyd

Foster And Lloyd reflect the current changes in Nashville. They're young, hip and haven't spent years paying dues but they do have talent. And RCA have let that talent flourish by giving the duo room and time. Their reward is the polished début, 'Foster And Lloyd'. Radney Foster (the one with the glasses) was the first of the duo to move to Nashville. Originally from Del Rio, Texas, he attended the University Of The South and playing in a local club one night was approached by a fellow who offered to introduce him to a producer friend in Nashville. Optimistic perhaps, but Foster took the gamble, waited on tables and pitched songs.

Eventually the new MTM Music Group took him on as a staff writer. It was there that he met Bill Lloyd. "My initial reaction to him (Foster) was the fact that he was one of the youngest songwriters out there and the fact that he had a little pony tail and these glasses made me think, 'He looks vaguely hip. I may end up writing with this guy'."

Bill Lloyd's musical inspiration was sixties rock, the British beat bands and bluegrass. He worked in New York and then put a band together in Kentucky before moving to Nashville in 1982 where he signed to MTM. Writing together they hit gold with the breakthrough song for The Sweethearts Of The Rodeo. Then Foster teamed up with Holly Dunn to write 'Love Someone Like Me' with Bill Lloyd playing guitar. RCA sensed talent and signed the duo.

"They didn't put any restrictions on us when we went in to make the record," Foster remembers. "They just said, 'You guys go in and make it any way you want'." A less confident pair might have crumbled under the freedom and responsibility. If the sessions failed they had only themselves to blame. But they didn't fail. *Rolling Stone* called their début, "An example of what's right in Nashville these days," and their first two singles made the top 10 in the *Billboard* charts.

New to the game they've quickly learned to compensate for each other's weakness and utilise their different strengths. "Radney is the primary singer and I have a lot more input as far as production is concerned," says Bill. If they have to describe it they'll call their music . . . "An amalgamation of roots rock, sixties pop and country all meshed together." Their sound recalls The Byrds, Eagles, Neil Young, Buck Owens and even a dash of Lennon and McCartney. But Foster's voice is country through and through and their own musical pot pourri is immediately identifiable as Foster And Lloyd, a rare feat for a new act.

They're almost the second wave of new country, less rock than Steve Earle, more pop than The Judds and they're in the enviable position of appealing to kids via college radio, the rock grapevine and the more hardcore country airwaves. But then times are changing for country radio as Lloyd enthuses, "Country music radio seems to be the one thing you can listen to without getting bored." Foster And Lloyd are a significant part of that diversity.

Vince Gill

Vince Gill has for years been touted as the man most likely to become a star. A well respected session player, his work has furthered the careers of numerous country artists from Rosanne Cash to Emmylou Harris and Bonnie Raitt. Recently he's become known as the husband of Janis Gill of Sweethearts Of The Rodeo Fame, but it surely can't be long before Vince Gill is a name in his own right.

Oklahoma born, Vince's first real musical experience came with a local bluegrass band, Mountain Smoke, which utilised his singing and guitar playing talents. His reputation spread and Bluegrass Alliance, which featured legendary pickers Sam Bush and Dan Crary, called him up. From there he worked with Byron Berline's Sundance on the West Coast.

Three albums with bluegrass rock band Pure Prairie League followed before he teamed up with Rodney Crowell. "One night when I was still with Byron Berline," recalls Gill, "we played the Troubadour in LA. I sang 'Til I Gain Control' and he came up and said, 'By the way I'm Rodney Crowell and I wrote that song.' When he left Emmylou's band he called me up to play with the Cherry Bombs."

Gill's high harmony singing (which still hadn't been sympathetically recorded) and dexterous guitar skills, marked him out as an in-demand player. But his solo recording deal came through old friend and one-time Cherry Bomb, Tony Brown, then handling A&R for RCA. In 1984 Gill recorded a six-song mini-LP with session ace Emory Gordy Jr. The title track, 'Turn Me Loose' was an immediate success and Gill won the Academy Of Country Music's Top New Male Vocalist Award for that year. A duet with Rosanne Cash, 'If It Weren't For Him' culled from his second album 'The Things That Matter' (RCA), went top 10 but Gill still wasn't the star the pundits had predicted.

Clearly Gill had everything going for him but that magic spark was eluding him. Vince opted to concentrate more on his writing and his relationship with Janis was perfectly expressed on the third album, 'The Way Back Home' (RCA), especially in one of Gill's most mature and well crafted songs, 'The Radio'. It came from personal experience. "It seems that's almost how Janis and I communicate these days. I turn on the radio and there she is. OK she may be far away but there she is." The album's title track again proved that Gill, beside his obvious musical gifts, can compose thoughtful and incisive lyrics. "It's about missing children. I have a daughter and I can't tell you what it does to me when she is not exactly where I think she is sometimes." But Gill has not let his instrumental wizardry slip, and on one track from 'The Way Back Home' he dazzles on banjo, mandolin and dobro.

Vince Gill has progressed from the cult ghetto of acoustic music to potential mainstream recording star but has refused to dilute his musical vision. Banjos and fiddle crop up frequently as does the high lonesome sound on the vocals. Gill has respect in country music circles, an asset probably worth far more than the fickle vagaries of stardom.

Jimmie Gilmore

Jimmie Gilmore, Joe Ely, Butch Hancock, Steve Wesson and Tony Pearson came together in Texas in the late sixties as The Flatlanders, a band still revered in country rock circles. They toured extensively and made one album, 'One Road More' which is now very hard to find. At the time Gilmore was the more developed artist among several budding talents and his vocals were stunning. His style was a throwback to Woody Guthrie and Jimmie Rodgers, a high pitched, nasally whine that sent shivers down the spine.

In the following years Joe Ely went on to major league success and Butch Hancock became well known as a writer, but Gilmore slipped from view. An intelligent and sensitive man he plunged headlong into the study of philosophy and Eastern religion while playing the odd club date around Austin, Texas. Music as a career, it seemed, was not a prior requirement but the late eighties see Gilmore making a comeback. He plays regularly in Texas and Europe and has signed to Hightone, Joe Ely's current label.

In 1988 Gilmore recorded 'Fair And Square' (Hightone), an excellent album produced by Ely and featuring fine tunes from old friend and collaborator Butch Hancock. If anyone can make it big time from Austin, Texas, it's going to be Jimmie Gilmore.

GIRLS NEXT DOOR,
LEFT TO RIGHT:
**CINDY, TAMMY,
DORIS AND DIANE**

The Girls Next Door

Something of a fabricated group, The Girls Next Door have added a new dimension to Nashville's female vocalist sound. Singing country as well as soul and forties swing, the girls refuse to be pigeonholed even though Nashville has taken them to its heart. In 1982 top Nashville producer Tommy West challenged session singer Doris King to find three other female vocalists to make a winning line-up.

King recruited Cindy Nixon (her father and uncle were the well known Nixon Brothers), Opryland singer Tammy Stephens, and Diane Williams. The self-titled début album for MTM Records show-cased the women's impressive vocal and harmony talents. More interesting was the choice and treatment of material which included pop classics done the Nashville way. The second album 'What A Girl Next Door Could Do' (MTM), further established the group as a healthy addition to a growing diversity of country music styles prevalent in Nashville and on country radio in the late eighties.

Nanci Griffith

Alongside new country cohorts Lyle Lovett, Steve Earle and Dwight Yoakam, Nanci Griffith has pioneered country music's move into college radio and a rock market. Griffith herself is far removed from rock music but as a singer songwriter she stands as an equal to the likes of pop poet Joni Mitchell. Griffith has a devoted following in Europe and a growing body of support across the United States.

The man who signed her to MCA, Tony Brown, believes that she has at least as much talent as Suzanne Vega and Tracy Chapman and can see no reason for her not to rival them in record sales. Griffith's brand of crossover is far removed from the genre breaking work of mid-seventies stars like Glen Campbell or Barbara Mandrell. Like the new traditionalists her music is rootsy, sparse and linked very closely to old-time styles.

Griffith first hit the headlines by writing Kathy Mattea's first big hit 'Love At The Five And Dime', but previous to that she'd spent over a decade in the clubs and recording studios of Texas. Nanci was raised in Texas, a middle class kid who fell for the music of Woody Guthrie, Hank Williams and Buddy Holly. Her first real influence was Texas folk singer Carolyn Hester. "She and Loretta Lynn really inspired me because they were women and kind of role models to me," she recalls. By the age of 14 she was playing Austin Honky Tonks. "I guess it was kind of young but I learned pretty quickly how to look after myself and you learn in those places how to write songs that'll make people listen. That's the secret."

Griffith continued her education at The University Of Texas where she developed a healthy appetite for books, Texas novels in particular. She taught kindergarten for a while but her reputation as a singer and performer was spreading and by the late seventies she was pursuing a music career full-time. She produced four of the finest independent label albums of the past decade, 'There's A Light Beyond These Woods', 'Poet In My Window', 'Once In A Very Blue Moon' and 'Last Of The True Believers'.

She seemed destined to live the life of the country renegade; a few well received albums, plenty of gigs and not too much money. She felt her music was, "Too folky for the traditional country establishment." Fortunately for Griffith country music was moving back to basics in the early eighties and Tony Brown, impressed by the sales of her indie albums and definitely a fan of her music, signed her to MCA. There was no pressure on her to conform. "When we made the first MCA album, 'Lone Star State Of Mind', they let me co-produce so I still had a major say in the sound."

Surrounded by fine players Griffith's album rang fresh and true around Nashville in 1987. Her vocals warble and the songs bite from tales like the farmers' plight in 'Trouble In The Fields' and the nostalgic 'There's A Light Beyond These Woods, Mary Margaret'. Her band sounds pure country but Griffith's vocals are unique and distinctive. "I like to call my music folk-a-billy, a mix of folk and hillbilly. A little bit of Woody Guthrie and a whole lotta Loretta Lynn," she claims.

As a writer Griffith's influences are more likely to be found on the pages of a novel than from her record collection. She's an avid reader and is frequently pictured clutching a novel on her album covers. She admits to near hero worship of Larry McMurtery and not content with ploughing through at least three novels a week, she's written two of her own. Like her prose her songs deal with small-town life in Texas. She deals with the little people – losers, lovers, dreamers and travellers. "Somehow this dream of America has gotten into people's minds. It's some deep desire to succeed and better yourself. But it often fails. It's that dilemma that I find fascinating."

Her second MCA album 'Little Love Affairs' is filled with vignettes and tales of love. She looks as an observer on relationships, both the successes and the failures. It was a more gentle album than 'Lone Star State Of Mind' but a fine work on its own terms.

Still, despite a high media profile, country radio failed to play Griffith's material with any great frequency. MCA moved her office affairs to LA in an attempt to market her more as a rock act, but that's not to say Griffith is leaving country music or Nashville. "I'm staying in Nashville and the music isn't going to change."

Her third album for MCA, 'One Fair Summer's Evening' recorded live at the Anderson's Fair in Houston, Texas, proves her point. It's a bare album, a songwriter's record that shows off her flowing guitar work, impassioned singing and intelligent writing. Songs old and new are given the troubadour treatment. Nanci Griffith is still something of a pioneer, her music stands or falls on her writing. So far the muse has not deserted her. Indeed Griffith's songs become more layered, and better crafted with every release.

☆ ★ ★ ★ ☆

Butch Hancock

Hancock is best known for his songwriting – his work was first picked up by Jerry Jeff Walker and more recently Joe Ely has bolstered his albums with Hancock material. He has been a major force behind the Texas music scene for nearly 20 years and with country music moving towards a more rootsy sound his writing talents should find wider acceptance. He was one of the legendary Flatlanders back in the early seventies alongside Joe Ely and Jimmie Gilmore. "There wasn't a whole lot to do in Lubbock and a bunch of us would hang out in coffee bars playing and singing. That's where I met Joe Ely."

But this was before the outlaw movement, before the success of Jerry Jeff Walker, Michael Murphey and Steve Fromholz and long before the Willie and Waylon 'outlaw' movement. Their music was strictly small-time with little potential for career building. Hancock went to college studying architecture and then travelled to the West Coast. "I was really influenced by the art of San Francisco, the architecture and the whole hippy thing was very creative. It influenced my later design work and it spurred me into writing lyrics and music."

Lying somewhere between Dylan and Woody Guthrie, Hancock's music developed quickly as he played around Texas once more. He concentrated on story

songs, writing on a host of subjects and capturing Texas characteristics with an uncanny knack. Left of centre and barely commercial, Hancock still picked up a large following, started his own record label, Rainlight, and has so far produced seven colourful albums.

Often working with players from Joe Ely's band and keeping his songs bitingly bare with just guitar, voice and harmonica, Hancock's music is always diverse and epic in its intentions. Not for him simple love songs, Hancock prefers to dig his teeth into philosophy and issues but never becomes pretentious. Like Dylan he makes major points with subtlety and understatement.

A 1985 album, 'Yella Rose' (Rainlight) saw him partnered by Marce LeCoutre, a hearty female vocalist, and the album rippled with melody and lyrical twists. The songs were also remarkably commercial and it seemed that Hancock could break out of the Texas ghetto into a mainstream country singer songwriter career. Typically however his 1986 follow-up album was a heavy concept album, 'Split And Flied II' (Rainlight). Like his friend Terry Allen, Hancock is in the fortunate position of having a fulfilling career outside of music. It may be frustrating for fans but that freedom ensures work of the highest artistic integrity.

Highway 101

Respected band manager Chuck Morris (he looks after The Nitty Gritty Dirt Band and Lyle Lovett among others) played a key role not just in taking Highway 101 to the top but in assembling the band in the first place. Morris spent two years planning the development of the sound he calls, "traditional country with a rock 'n' roll backbeat." Manufactured they may be but Highway 101 sound more 'real' than a host of rock or country bands who developed in the usual way. They re-create their studio sound perfectly on stage – gutsy guitars, heavy rock drumming and blaring vocals from lead singer Paulette Carlson. If these are the results of careful auditioning and planning then Morris may have hit on a winning formula.

The band was assembled around Paulette Carlson one-time writer for the Oak Ridge Boys' publishing company who demoed some songs for an RCA singles deal. Nothing came of it but when Morris heard her he realised he'd found the lynchpin for his band idea. Next he called on LA drummer Cactus Moser, a respected beat merchant who had worked for Chris Hillman, Bernie Leadon, Jennifer Warnes and Johnny Rivers. (He was also something of a film star, having backed Rodney Dangerfield on the 'Twist And Shout' sequence in the Hollywood comedy *Back To School*). Friendships and the grapevine recruited bass player Curtis Stone (son of legendary forties West Coast country musician Cliffie Stone), whose harmonies have lifted recordings by Tennessee Ernie Ford and Freddie Hart among others. Guitarist Jack Daniels also played with Freddie Hart and won a reputation as a top session player, often working with the likes of Albert Lee and Glen D. Hardin.

Recalling the group's beginnings drummer Moser remembers that . . . "I'd known Chuck for years and he'd often spoken about his plan for a special kind of band, but he was never clear what kind of band. But when we started to play together everything fell into place." Initially Warner Bros gave Morris's fledgling band a singles deal and while the first effort 'Some Find Love' bombed, their second attempt, 'The Bed You Made For Me', a Carlson original, hit the country top five. Morris's plan had worked and Warners quickly signed Highway 101. Their eponymous début album went top 10 within a few weeks of release.

44

Carlson's impressive vocals, crisp, rocky and clear, proved the perfect front for a rock band playing country. They had the power of pop and the grace of country. Allied to impressive harmonies and great songs, their sound quickly saw them as one of the top country bands and it was no surprise that they picked up the 1988 Country Music Association's Award for Best Group. A second album, 'Highway 101(2)' (Warners) consolidated their position with a barrage of top tunes and a healthy dose of steamy guitar-based country.

Having spent so many years backing rock acts some of Highway 101's players have found live shows a challenge, restraining themselves when they might want to 'rock out' as Moser puts it. But that ability to change gear on stage has given the band an edge over their rivals. Says Stone, "I feel like we've done something very important and taken the roots of country music, and don't forget rock 'n' roll came out of country, and made them contemporary."

Becky Hobbs

Hobbs plays modern honky tonk. A flailing piano player, she sings with gusto and, while some of her performances may lack a considered subtlety, her all-out style makes her one of the most powerful and dynamic performers in Nashville. Her recent MTM début album, 'All Keyed Up' is filled to the brim with rolling piano, twangy guitar and vocals of which Janis Joplin would have been proud.

Like so many of Nashville's new stars, Hobbs' story has been long and at times weary. "Well, I was raised in Oklahoma and my dad was a real big music fan and he bought me a piano when I was nine-years-old. In the fifties I got into rock 'n' roll, you know Jerry Lee Lewis, Rick Nelson and all that stuff." In high school Becky played with an all-girl band, Sir Prize Package, learning the art of performance and delivering a song. From there she moved to Tulsa, spent a year at university before heading for Baton Rouge and a piano and singing job with local band Swamp Fox. The band took her to LA but broke up in 1973. "It was after that I really got into country music in LA. I cut an album for MCA which wasn't very good."

Becky's career as a songwriter was boosted after Helen Reddy covered one of her songs, but things were slow until publisher Al Gallico won her a deal with Mercury in Nashville.

Hobbs had six chart singles but still made no real headway as a major solo star, though she was finding some support in Nashville. Moe Bandy expressed a desire to work with her and their top 10 duet won Hobbs a deal with EMI/America where she scored with a top selling single, 'Hottest Ex In Texas'. Fortunately, even though solo success eluded her, Hobbs built a reputation as a writer, her songs being recorded by country heavyweights Emmylou Harris, Glen Campbell, John Anderson, Janie Fricke and others. With country music looking again to its roots and with female acts outgunning the men, Hobbs was signed on a solo basis to MTM. Steve Earle guitar-man Richard Bennet produced the album and contributed killer guitar solos. Hobbs handled piano and vocals with rare enthusiasm and musical mastery.

In a music industry that can at times take itself too seriously, Hobbs is a refreshing down-home addition who adds spark and sparkle to any show.

☆ ★ ★ ★ ☆

Michael Johnson

Michael Johnson has been recording in Nashville studios since the early seventies but remained largely unknown to the country music fraternity. He played folk music in the sixties and leaned towards adult pop in the late seventies, scoring a pop hit with 'Bluer Than Blue'. As Nashville opened up he moved towards country and recorded a top 10 hit with Sylvia, 'I Love You By Heart', and moved on to record two RCA albums, 'Wings' and 'That's That'.

He's still on the folk side of country but with Nanci Griffith and Lyle Lovett doing good business with a similar style, he's enjoying a purple patch in a career that dates back to 1964 when he won a folk singing contest at Colorado State College. The prize was an Epic recording contract. Nothing happened however and Johnson spent a year in Spain studying classical guitar before returning to join the Chad Mitchell Trio alongside John Denver. Caught up in the mid-sixties folk boom he recorded an album for Atlantic, 'This Is A Breeze', but it failed to capture the public's imagination. He then made albums on his own Sanskrit label before moving to Nashville and finding work as a session player.

Johnson found country music eighties-style more to his folk leanings, his recordings feature Johnson's vocals and guitar well up-front in the mix. Teamed with Judds producer Brent Maher, Johnson produced a fine album with 'That's That', a stripped back sound that lets the lyrical intelligence and craftsmanlike singing and playing rise to the top.

As country music broadens its horizons to embrace jazz, soul and folk roots then artists like Michael Johnson will contribute a great deal.

David Lynn Jones

Jones is more rock than many of his counterparts but his début album, 'Hard Times On Easy Street' (Polygram) has won great support from the country fraternity.

Lynn Jones has been playing since 1970, sometimes in Nashville, sometimes in Texas, learning his craft, honing his individual style. The new mood in Nashville gave him his major label chance in the late eighties and his début album, with Springsteen and Dylan overtones, is conclusive proof that his time is about to come.

The Judds (Wynonna And Naomi)

Mother and daughter duo The Judds are a phenomenon in modern country music. They've sold millions of records (including more than 15 number one singles), captured the public's imagination with their *Dynasty* looks and impressed country and rock critics with their harmony based old-time traditional mountain music. Alongside Ricky Skaggs The Judds opened the doors for new country. Their stripped down sound, predominantly acoustic and optimistic but down-home lyrics, gave Nashville a shake up in 1984. Theirs was a free-flowing back-to-the-roots sound that Nashville had lost sight of in the seventies.

The Judds did the right thing at the right time but most importantly they did it very well. They may have lived in California for a while but essentially daughter Wynonna and mother Naomi (real names Diana and Christina – they changed when a new start beckoned after Diana's divorce and a move from Hollywood back to Kentucky) are mountain people.

"I grew up in California and I was a typical *Brady Bunch* kid but we moved to Kentucky when I was 13-years-old," Wynonna remembers. "That's where country music comes from – the Appalachian Mountains. I lived with people who didn't know what it was like in the outside world. If I took them to New York, it'd be like *Crocodile Dundee*. But I discovered bluegrass. It was a real education for me, country music is about real people in real life situations and it's very emotional."

While Wynonna was discovering the joys of hillbilly music, mother Naomi was struggling to support her family as a nurse. Without a TV at home they sang for fun, unwittingly developing a vocal style that would win them a contract with RCA. Wynonna clearly had talent, her voice impressed her mother and the judges at a high school talent contest. While nursing the daughter of top producer Brent Maher, Naomi took the opportunity of passing on a cheaply made demo tape of her and Wynonna. Maher loved the sound, rough perhaps but crammed with potential. In no time at all the duo were signed to RCA and had two 1984 number ones, 'Mama He's Crazy' and 'Why Not Me'.

Their début mini-album, 'The Judds' (RCA), kicked off an impressive recording record. Their four full-size albums, 'Why Not Me', 'Rockin' With The Rhythm', 'Heartlands' (RCA, USA) 'Give A Little Love' (RCA, UK) and 'Greatest Hits' have remained in the charts since they were released, and the glamorous duo have won the Country Music Association's prestigious Vocal Group Of The Year Award for more than three years running.

Duos are commonplace in country music but a mother and daughter pairing is somewhat unusual. Fortunately Wynonna has found no difficulties working with her mother. "It's a bit of a drag sometimes when she tells me to go tidy my room when we're on the road but really we get on great, we're more like friends than anything." Naomi's maturity has given the women an air of confidence and grooming and cajoled Wynonna into possibly the finest female country singer around. Should she attempt rock she'd probably be a great success; her voice is at home with traditional country or upbeat numbers, and this is especially evident in live shows.

Wynonna grew up listening to West Coast rock and these days immerses herself in Bruce Hornsby, Bonnie Raitt, Tracy Chapman and even 'new age' music. A recent appearance on stage with Bono from U2 was, she says, a high point in her career. Whether or not Wynonna Judd pursues a solo career in future years, at present The Judds have hit on a winning formula. The years spent singing around the house have given the two women a great advantage over most music acts. They sound completely

at ease with each other's style and phrasing. They sing as one, although behind the scenes, Brent Maher might be counted as the third Judd. His production is always crystal clear and veers just to the right side of slushy on sentimental numbers.

Primarily acoustic, the band avoids tiresome lead guitar clichés that drag so many bands down. On the rock songs they swing with the best but they're equally at home with old-time tear jerkers.

Live or on video another Judds factor comes into play – the look. Mixing down-home sentiment with high fashion may not be new, but The Judds have dragged country music costumes into the eighties. It's the Hollywood connection. "But remember," says Wynonna defiantly, "we had our first hit from radio when nobody knew what we looked like. It's the music that counts not the make up and hair-dos. Anyway it can work against us. When we toured with Neil Young I felt so out of place and real scared of what all these punks in the audience would think. But they listened to the songs and liked us."

TV producers haven't missed the point either. The Judds' personalities plus looks would make perfect television and a suitable format is currently being sought. With their evident talent and advantages, The Judds' success story should know no bounds.

☆　★　★　★　☆

k.d. Lang

In 1987 k.d. Lang was being hailed as a promising newcomer, an addition to the growing interest in the rock roots of country music. In 1988 she recorded a straight country album in Nashville with legendary producer Owen Bradley (the man responsible for Patsy Cline's production) and artists like Brenda Lee and Kitty Wells were singing her praises. She's already proved she can tackle country music from both a rock perspective and a pure country angle, all in the space of two albums.

k.d. Lang has played a key role in taking country music to a younger audience. Her appearance is hip – a cropped hair cut and sombre black outfits are the norm. She adopts the rock star's pose of performing in shades. A friend of Roy Orbison's she appeared on a 1988 video celebrating the Big O's career alongside Bruce Springsteen, Jackson Browne, Elvis Costello and other rock mainstays. If anyone can draw the youth market in to country music it's k.d. Lang.

Hailing from Consort, Alberta, in Canada ("The most beautiful country in the World" – k.d. Lang) Kathy Dawn as she was known, began learning piano at just seven-years-old. At 10 she picked up a guitar and spent her teenage years writing songs. She absorbed country music. "Just because I lived in Canada didn't mean there wasn't any country music. We had it all plus some good Canadian artists. But I can still remember the thrill of hearing Loretta Lynn and Patsy Cline."

It wasn't long before Lang was devoting her time to playing music. "I really enjoy singing and performing. I get a little nervous but nothing can match the feeling of losing yourself in a song on-stage. I guess I'm only really happy when I'm singing."

And so she began to work with bands and writing country influenced material. By 1983 she had her own country band, The Reclines. In 1984 they topped a series of hugely popular concerts with an independently produced album, 'A Truly Western Experience' (Bumstead Records) which led to a contract with Sire Records and an album, 'Angel With A Lariat' produced by Dave Edmunds. *Rolling Stone* called it . . . "An auspicious début on a major label by an artist whose performance is already legendary." There was an element of cowpunk about the album – the band played loud and sometimes a little rough and Lang's vocals cut sharp like a switch-blade through a swell of electric noise. It wasn't a mainstream Nashville country radio album by any means but it did win her friends from the rock world and plenty of media attention.

Lang and her band toured heavily for 10 months. For those expecting a similar follow-up album, her second record for Sire, 'Shadowlands' was quite a shock. Lang had always been a "Patsy Cline fanatic" and she knew what she wanted for her album. She coaxed producer Owen Bradley out of semi-retirement and embarked on a "real wonderful experience. You see I'd listened to all those Patsy Cline records and the sound was so great that after a while I became just as much a fan of Owen Bradley as Patsy Cline. It was daunting working with him, but he's a great guy and put me at ease very quickly." Bradley was just as excited about the project as the young Canadian. "I'd had a heart attack not long before and working with k.d. was like an elixir. There's something about hearing a really great singer that gets the blood going again. She made me remember what had always been exciting about being in the studio. I guess you could say she made it fun again."

Fun aside, 'Shadowland' came out a most accomplished piece. "There's a bit of everything in there from pure fifties country to kind of big band things and some pop. I wanted to make the record as a tribute to a great producer as much as anything and everybody involved worked to the highest standard."

One track stands out as much for the line-up as the performance, 'The Honky Tonk Angels Medley' featuring Kitty Wells, Loretta Lynn and Brenda Lee. "Of course I was nervous," says Lang. "I'd grown up looking up to those women but they were fine about it. We just a had laugh and a good time."

k.d. Lang is cool, confident and eager to learn. "I watched Owen Bradley pretty close during those sessions and I really want to produce my own records. I'm sure I can manage it now. I mean I don't enjoy all the technical stuff but to be able to feel that you've created a whole sound is wonderful. That's definitely the direction I want to follow."

Patty Loveless

More traditionally minded than some of her MCA stablemates, Patty Loveless bridges the gap between pre-seventies country and progressive country with great finesse. Her band sounds up to the minute and her songs ring true with eighties notions, but vocally

she's reminiscent of the old-time sound, definitely more Loretta Lynn than Janie Fricke. With three albums under her belt and around 15 years of touring experience to her name, Loveless will be a new country mainstay for some time to come.

Loveless comes from Pikeville, Kentucky, the town that also gave country music Dwight Yoakam. As a teenager her family moved to Louisville so her father could receive treatment for a serious coal mining induced illness. Her brother Roger Ramey (now her manager) introduced her to local country music shows. Already a good singer she quickly learned songs and began performing with Roger on jamborees. Ramey was never outstanding vocally and he knew it. But Patty had a gift and when she was just 14 the pair drove the 150 miles to Nashville armed with around 30 songs. Confidently they walked into Porter Waggoner's office and played some to him. Patty's career had begun. The Wilburn brothers heard her sing and invited her on to their show to replace Loretta Lynn.

For the next few years Patty Loveless spent her winters at school in Louisville and her summers in Nashville. She was still considered too young for a recording career and when she married Terry Lovelace, The Wilburns' drummer, she dropped out of the Nashville scene and retreated to North Carolina. "When I got married I kinda left country music as a career," she recalls. "But I began singing with bands again, mostly rock and pop. But it was good for my voice, I learned how to project and work an audience."

Her real musical love was still traditional mountain music and when Nashville once again opened up to the old-time sounds Loveless (a variation on her now ex-husband's name Lovelace . . . "I thought people might get the wrong idea in Nashville if I was called Lovelace, they might think I was related to Linda or something,") tried Nashville again. Roger Ramey helped out by getting a demo tape to Tony Brown at MCA. He played the tape to old friend and in-demand player and producer, Emery Gordy Jr, who was immediately struck by the power in the voice and the beauty of Patty's high lonesome mountain singing.

The début album, 'Patty Loveless' (MCA) featured a contemporary and slick sleeve that immediately signalled her as a potential member of the new country clan. The sound was, as Loveless described it, "traditional country with a little edge." In fact it had a lot of edge with Patty's vocals falling somewhere between the cool mountain grace of Loretta Lynn and the rock twang of Rosanne Cash. The songs on the album were some of the best around, notably a rocking version of Steve Earle's 'Some Blue Moons Ago' (about which Earle remarked, "That's the only cover version of any of my songs that I think is any good, she's got a fine voice."). There was also a nod towards Texas with the dance-hall feel of 'Lonely Days, Lonely Nights' and the simplicity of one of Guy Clark's better tunes, 'You Are Everything'.

As an album her début was a cohesive unit rather than a vehicle for several singles. A sign perhaps that while Loveless wouldn't achieve overnight celebrity status, she would become a long-term artist, consistently producing well crafted records.

On the strength of her début album Loveless toured heavily opening shows for George Jones, Reba McEntire, Randy Travis and The Judds. A visit to the Wembley Festival in England in 1987 won her great European acclaim, as did a repeat visit the following year. The second album, 'If My Heart Had Windows', again proved Loveless to be a consummate album artist. Nashville's best new writer contributed material but once more it was Loveless' vocal maturity and interpretive talents that shone through.

The next album, 'Honky Tonk Angels' (MCA), improved on both previous albums. Tony Brown producing on his own, rather than with Emery Gordy Jr.

Brown seems to have the Midas touch these days (ask Lyle Lovett, Nanci Griffith, Steve Earle or Rodney Crowell) and the overall sound is bright, punchy and very sympathetic to Loveless' vocals. Rodney Crowell contributes some brooding harmonies and with players of the calibre of Albert Lee and Mark O'Connor chipping in where necessary, the album immediately won comparisons with the early work of Emmylou Harris.

Loveless brings a fresh voice to country music - traditional but always ready to rock 'n' roll. "I love country but it's fun to really let go sometimes. I think that's what gives my records that distinctive sound, that edge." She also feels far happier coming across as a rocker on-stage than a sequined country doll. "Nothing against those women who get all dressed up, like Dolly, I mean Dolly helped me out so much when I was starting out. But I'm a down to earth person and I like to sing in my everyday clothes."

Lyle Lovett

He may be left of centre by Nashville standards but the folksy, jazzy twang of Lyle Lovett is probably as well known outside the country field as any of the newer country acts. Praised to the hilt by the rock press and very popular on the college radio circuit, Lovett is insuring that his somewhat cornball name is known across the States. His two albums, a self-titled début on MCA and a progressive follow-up, 'Pontiac' (MCA), have won him a reputation as an individual creator, an adventurous artist amongst a gang of traditionalists.

Originally from Texas, Lovett left the farming areas where he was raised to attend the Texas A&M University in Houston. By day he majored in journalism, by night he hung out in local bars and clubs soaking up the wordy twists of the troubadours, thrilling to their flowing picking on acoustic guitars. He struck up a performer's friendship with Nanci Griffith (he's pictured on one of her early album covers) and began performing and writing himself. "I started doing covers but I was never a good enough singer to do Merle Haggard tunes, so I realised that I had to do my own. If I'd been a better singer or player maybe I'd have never started writing."

But write he did until 1984 when he headed for Nashville with a four-track demo tape which publishers ASCAP loved. Old friend Guy Clark helped Lyle out and passed a tape to Tony Brown at MCA. "Tony was great," says Lovett. "Basically he got me the deal with MCA and produced the album. He gave us enough rope to hang ourselves." Brown recognised that Lovett's great advantage was his individuality. He looked odd, the songs weren't straight down-the-line country and his voice sounded more Tom Waits than George Jones. Even the band on the first album came from an unlikely place. "I ran into this band in Phoenix of all places, a real young band. And most of them were into jazz. So the sound on the record really developed from them. I used a cello player which is pretty unusual in country music, but I like to try different things."

For 'Pontiac' Lovett reached back into Texas' musical heritage and played around with swing, country and blues. "I guess the album's a kind of a blues thing. Certainly more so than the first album. And it was the same band only we also used Steve Earle's drummer to give it a bit more punch."

Lovett's a throwback to the early seventies cosmic cowboys, but he's no re-hasher of previously tried ideas. He's more at home in a songwriter's club than, "some dance hall or honky tonk where they really want dance music." He likes people to sit and listen. "I don't think my songs are heavy at all, but they're not straight country. I'd like to think that the songs stand up to several listenings."

Lovett's albums have thrown the marketing department of MCA Records into a flurry. Some singles are directed at country radio, others at jazz, some to blues and R&B. And while that has possibly confused the public, Lovett's diversity of styles is also his greatest asset. He hasn't been hailed as some kind of a country music saviour nor has he announced himself a hillbilly prophet. He's an intelligent man, low-key, slow of speech but swift of thought. His songs tackle topics from varied and unusual angles. "The only thing I've got going for me really is my point of view," he says. As befits a trained reporter, Lovett's songs pick out the unusual from the commonplace. On 'Pontiac' he writes about broken marriages from an angle of bitter irony with a 'Chip kicker redneck woman' and a host of oddball but believable characters.

Lovett is a street corner poet, a man who grew up on early seventies Texas songwriters like Guy Clark, Townes Van Zandt and Jerry Jeff Walker, especially Jerry Jeff "who was a major influence on me when I was 17 or 18-years-old." Like his mentors, Lovett sees with a poet's eye and writes with a jaunty turn of phrase, notably on 'God Will'. But unlike his predecessors Lovett is prepared to experiment musically. He's just as happy with beat generation, finger-popping jazz as he is with dusty home-on-the-range Texas ballads. And what is most staggering is that he manages to blend his stylistic influences into an identifiable whole. Even when he plays swing or jazz it still sounds like Lyle Lovett.

Lovett still can't believe his success. "You know I have people sending me tapes, thinking that I can help them out and I don't even feel that I've established myself yet." Lovett is smart, a man with two degrees, who is all set to take country music out of that mythical redneck ghetto and introduce the beauty and power of Texas music to a vast number of country and rock fans.

Shelby Lynne

Most country artists spend years struggling, paying their dues and supporting their musical ambitions with various day jobs. Others find overnight success. Time will tell how successful Shelby Lynne is destined to be, but so far her musical career has progressed with speed and not a little good fortune.

Shelby, from Jackson, Alabama, auditioned for a spot on Opryland at Mobile. Unfortunately she was turned down but a young songwriter heard her at the audition and asked her to sing on a demo of one of his own songs. The songwriter brought the tapes to Nashville with him and within two weeks Shelby Lynne was booked on to a local TV show, *Nashville Now*. Legendary producer Billy Sherill (the man behind Tammy Wynette's success) saw the 19-year-old and was immediately struck by her vocals and presence. His influence led to a contract with Epic Records.

Her first single, a duet with George Jones, 'If I Could Bottle This Up', set her on her way to a hectic touring schedule playing with, among others, George Jones, Randy Travis, Ricky Van Shelton and even an appearance at the Opry with Roy Acuff. Respected music critic Robert Oermann wrote in the *Nashville Tennesseean* after seeing Lynne at Fan Fair, "A star was born when young Alabaman Shelby Lynne took the microphone and startled the audience with her flame-thrower delivery." So far Lynne has taken her overnight successes in her stride. "Real pressure," she says, "is a fiddling convention when you have to win the solo voice competition because you need 25 dollars."

☆ ★ ★ ★ ☆

Kathy Mattea

One of the finest singers in country music, Mattea came to Nashville and won a recording contract with Mercury just before Ricky Skaggs and The Judds proved that traditional country could be commercial. Her early efforts were rather slushy and sentimental but, as Nashville responded to the back to basics approach, so did Mattea and her producer Allen Reynolds, and she's ridden through the eighties as one of progressive country music's most talented artists.

Raised in Cross Lanes, Virginia, Mattea played and sang a whole range of music styles in high school. At university she joined a bluegrass band called Pennsboro and set her heart on a career in country music. In the late seventies she moved to Nashville to try her luck and found work as a tour guide at the Country Music Hall Of Fame. "Oh that was great. I met a lot of people and learned so much about country music. And it was good learning how to deal with the public because the same people who were going around the Hall Of Fame were attending country music concerts, so in a way I was learning how to communicate."

Mattea kept up her singing by working on demos and back-up vocals for touring acts. Slowly her vocal talents won the attention of Polygram Records who signed her to their Mercury label in 1983. But this was before the gates had opened for country music's female artists and Mattea's first self-titled album faded pretty quickly. It was a middle of the road contemporary sounding album, a throwback to the country pop records of the seventies. "There wasn't enough of the traditional sound on that album, but we weren't sure whether people would go for that sound at that time," remembers Mattea.

Her second album, 'From The Heart' (Mercury), released in 1985, was far closer to the mark and the hits started coming. Like Patty Loveless, Mattea's career built slowly but steadily, always more of an album artist than a quick fire singles merchant. After her second album, *People* magazine called her, "Unequalled among her generation of country singers." Working closely with producer Allen Reynolds (who directed Crystal Gale to superstardom) Mattea continued to improve and mature as a performer and in the studio.

The next album, 'Walk The Way The Wind Blows' was far less polished. It was a sound Mattea had been after for a while. "I was very choosy about the songs we

cut on that album. Unless they affected me on a gut level they weren't accepted. And we also took more time, which gave us more chances to find the right songs." 'Love At The Five And Dime' (a Nanci Griffith tune that saw Mattea at the top of the singles chart for the first time) came out of that process.

Mattea was now a major league artist and the follow-up album, 'Untasted Honey', continued the progression but this time saw Mattea attempting a mix of styles. There's a jazz and pop tinge to several numbers, but it's still rootsy and never slick for the sake of it. "You see I like so many kinds of music. And I've sung all kinds. In college I did choral and show music, then I played with a bluegrass band and I also dabbled with folk kind of things - Neil Young sort of things." As a result Mattea's albums appeal to a broad base of record buyers from the mainstream to new traditionalist fans.

Mattea admits that at one time she thought too much about what the audience wanted. "After a while I began to think I'm going to do it my way. And if it fouls up at least it's my mistake. And as soon as I put that kind of selfish attitude into operation my music improved and my records got successful. It makes me feel a lot more like an artist rather than just a good singer."

As far as writing goes Mattea still feels very nervous. "I do write and I want to write but most of my songs aren't very good. And on top of that I just don't get the time. It's hard enough being on the road so much that leading a normal life is hard. When I get back home for a couple of days I have so many things to do and people to see that the last thing on my list is writing songs. But it is a skill I want to develop."

THE McCARTERS,
LEFT TO RIGHT:
TERESA, JENNIFER
AND LISA

The McCarters

It's not often that a début album causes as much stir in Music City as did The McCarter's first Warner Bros album, 'The Gift'. The three sisters, Jennifer, Teresa and Lisa sing with a dynamic freshness - mountain harmonies laced with energy and power.

The sisters from Sevierville in the Smoky Mountains grew up surrounded by country music and made their first venture into show business via clog dancing. Eldest sister Jennifer was a great fan of the clogging shown on the *Grand Ole Opry* television shows. Joined by her sisters, twins Teresa and Lisa, the threesome learned their routines from watching television and practising to old Bill Monroe tunes. Soon their skills were enough to warrant them a regular spot on local TV. Talent scouts marked them down as having star quality but since the girls were still only nine and 11-years-old, contracts were premature.

Jennifer again took the lead in moving into music, learning to play guitar at 14 with the twins adding harmonies. The sound was good and the McCarter sisters began travelling to Pigeon Forge, to play on street corners for tips. They began to pick up engagements around Tennessee but never thought their style could prove nationally popular until they stumbled across a Randy Travis record.

Innocently ignorant of the machinations of the music business Jennifer tracked down Randy Travis' producer, Kyle Lehning and called him up. "I took it upon myself to call Kyle Lehning. And I called him two weeks in a row every day and asked him to listen to us audition 'cos we didn't have any demos."

Eventually Lehning gave way to Jennifer's persistent calling and granted them 15 minutes of his time. Then he contacted both Warners and Capitol, recommending the sisters for a recording contract. The Randy Travis connection came into play, the girls chose to go with Warners, and in January 1987 they left home for Nashville. "Mama was real sad when we left but she knows that's what we always wanted all our lives," says Jennifer.

The record company brought in some top players for their album, notably Carl Jackson and respected producers Paul Worley and Ed Seay. The results were first class and a début single, 'Timeless And True Love', went top five. Jennifer also proved herself an able songwriter with her heartfelt collaboration with Carl Jackson, 'Letter From Home'. Moreover the women proved themselves adept at live shows and video. So impressed was Dolly Parton, a fellow Smoky Mountains native, that she personally invited the McCarters to appear on her network TV show. Live the group are both powerful and charming, and they put across an infectious enthusiasm. The début album won praise from all sections of the media and looks to have introduced a new star package to country music.

Reba McEntire

Reba McEntire was the first of the new breed of female country artists to break through in Nashville. For 10 years now she has produced consistently high quality albums and picked up several gold albums and a vast collection of industry awards.

She moved from Mercury Records to MCA, telling *Billboard* at the time that . . . "We're going traditional country. No I'll take that back . . . we want to go new country. We're wanting to go new Loretta Lynn - to get new pickers, young pickers who are like me and want to stay country." Since then she's gone on to become not just one of the top vocalists in Nashville but in 1988 she reached the top 10 in a Gallup youth survey, naming her ahead of Pat Benatar, Cyndi Lauper and Stevie Nicks.

Born in Oklahoma in 1954, the daughter of a world champion steer roper, Reba joined a country band while still in the ninth grade. She planned to become a school teacher and enrolled at South-Eastern Oklahoma State University but music came first. In 1974 she was asked to sing the national anthem at the National Rodeo Finals where she impressed Red Seagall who helped her make a demo tape and win a deal with Mercury in Nashville. Her first single, 'I Don't Want To Be A One Night Stand', was released in 1976 but only a duet with Jacky Ward made the top 20.

Her 1978 début album illustrated McEntire's soulful flame-throwing vocals. She played old-time country but came over every inch a modern woman. "It's still pretty unusual to hear a woman sing a song about having an affair or standing up for herself. To me that's what hard country is all about - the freedom to say things you can't say on other more pop-oriented kinds of country music."

McEntire's move to MCA in 1984 pushed her from top flight country artist to star status. She co-produced her albums with veteran producer Jimmy Bowen, filled out shows with exciting stage craft and even played Las Vegas. Her first three singles for MCA, 'Just A Little Love', 'He Broke Your Mem'ry Last Night' and 'How Blue' all went top 20 and in October 1984 she won her first Country Music Association award for female vocalist of the year. She repeated her win the following year, a feat only matched by Dolly Parton, Barbara Mandrell and Loretta Lynn.

Not content with joining such illustrious company, she won the award again in 1986 and 1987, a unique achievement. McEntire clearly acted as a role model for many female artists who have followed her but none have matched her power on-stage. The redhead can belt out a song where needs be or glide graceful and sweet through a ballad. She has an eerie ability to set her voice just on the edge of heartbreak without falling foul of slushy sentimentality. Moreover, she carved herself a niche with songs that dealt with issues from a woman's point of view.

Her last four albums, 'The Last One To Know', 'Greatest Hits', 'What Am I Gonna Do About You?' and 'Whoever's In New England' have each sold more than half a million copies. Her 1988 album 'Reba' was filled with excellent love songs, all looking at relationships from a different angle. 'New Fool At An Old Game' is a telling account of second-time-around nerves. McEntire even has the audacity to tackle an Aretha Franklin classic, 'Respect' but comes away having added her own stamp and with no fears of failing to add anything new to an old, much-loved song.

'Reba' doesn't include any of McEntire's own songs. "We were looking for old good music and new good music and none of my stuff even came close to what I was offered. When I select songs, I don't care who writes them or publishes them. I go for the best." Indeed she does.

Dana McVicker

With a début album on Capitol that positively fizzes with country purity and rock 'n' roll roots, Dana McVicker has finally arrived as a recording artist. Long-time Nashville club performer, McVicker has proved that persistence and talent can win out.

A native of Baltimore, Maryland, Dana grew up in Philippi, West Virginia, but soon left the south for Florida where her father worked at Cape Canaveral. She was something of a child prodigy as far as music was concerned and by the time she was 17 she was performing throughout the south-east with a band, Red Pony Express. She gained plenty of experience on the road but it was a performance at the famed Stockyard Restaurant in Nashville that launched her recording career. Stockyard

OPPOSITE:
REBA McENTYRE.

owner Buddy Killen, also an influential music industry executive and owner of Tree International publishing, liked what he heard and signed her to regular work singing on demo sessions. An appearance on the TV show *Star Search* did her no harm at all but it was her demo work that really brought her to the attention of Capitol records.

Meanwhile she played with a local band called Paradise but left when Capitol offered her a deal. Bud Logan, a producer well known to Capitol through his ground-breaking work with T. Graham Brown was invited to produce the album. McVicker found the experience rewarding. "Bud pulls the best from you. He's soft spoken, yet not easily satisfied. He keeps you working to get your very best," she says.

Recorded in Nashville and Muscle Shoals, Alabama, the album utilised a selection of country music's finest musicians: Owen Hale and Larrie Londin on drums, Joe Osborn and Michael Rhodes on bass, Steve Nathan on keyboards and Mark Cassavetes and Brent Rowanon on guitar.

Not surprisingly, it's the vocals from Dana that stand out. Lying somewhere between Brenda Lee and Loretta Lynn, with a dash of southern soul, McVicker seems incapable of a half-hearted performance. She lives every song, savours every line and lingers on every note. She trembles through the Harlan Howard/Ron Peterson classic, 'I'm Loving The Wrong Man Again' but proves she can cut loose with a rocky rendition of 'Rock A Bye Heart' penned by Skip Ewing and Michael White. McVicker's delivery may not be subtle but if country music wants a blockbusting female vocalist it need look no further than this woman from Florida.

Donna Meade

Donna Meade became a well known Nashville entertainer during the eighties, performing regularly in local night clubs. More mainstream than some of the new artists signed in 1988 in Nashville, Meade has her own style, an electric fusion of straight country, a little pop, plenty of R&B and a hint of blues and gospel. Her début album, 'Love's Last Stand' gives vent to her remarkable vocal abilities as well as throwing in a number of musical styles.

All of Donna's family in Richmond, Virginia, were musical and from a young age she was adept on drums, bass, guitar and piano. At 17 she formed her own band, Country Roads, and performed at military bases across the United States. She was named Virginia's Female Artist Of The Year from 1977 to 1980. Winning competitions appealed to Meade and she was a top five finalist in the Miss Richmond Pageant and was voted Miss Congeniality in the Miss Virginia Pageant.

As the decade turned she moved to Nashville and found plenty of work in the nightclubs. A long-term contract in the Stockyard Restaurant won her many fans and also brought her into contact with owner Buddy Killen who set industry wheels in motion for her writing and recording ambitions.

In 1986 Donna signed a writer's contract with Tree International and in 1987 began work in the studio with Buddy Killen behind the desk. "Buddy was an old friend of Steve Popovich at Mercury and he recommended me, I guess that's how the record deal happened." The album included a number of stylistic influences (Meade cites Loretta Lynn, Patsy Cline, Ray Charles and Aretha Franklin as her musical heroes). Ballads on 'Be Serious' and 'From A Distance'; R&B on 'Congratulations'; and classic country on Harlan Howard's 'The Chokin' Kind' make up an album on which the production is clean and high-powered, thanks in the main to the appearance of the Muscle Shoals Horns.

With Nashville embracing new traditionalists, progressive singer songwriters and pop tinged R&B, influenced by artists like T. Graham Brown and Donna Meade, the musical pie looks juicy and appetising.

Michael Martin Murphey

Murphey is a survivor, a pioneer of cosmic country back in the early seventies, a mainstream artist later that decade, who now infuses roots and energy into a musical style that is every bit as exciting as the music of the younger pretenders. His longevity and determination have certainly paid off for Murphey is currently one of the hottest acts in country music.

A native Texan, Murphey was raised on the music of Hank Williams, Bob Wills and Woody Guthrie. At UCLA he played with pop outfit The Lewis And Clark Expedition with Boomer Castelman. Murphey lived in the Mojave desert and wrote songs for Kenny Rogers, Flatt and Scruggs and the fledgling Nitty Gritty Dirt Band. Fellow Texan and friend Mike Nesmith, one of sixties pop idols The Monkees, recorded Murphey's 'What Am I Doin' Hangin' Round' – one of The Monkees' finest musical achievements. The success of that song gave Murphey a writing contract with Screen Gems and he settled into life in the LA singer songwriter scene, alongside artists who would become The Eagles, Crosby Stills, Nash And Young and others.

In 1971 Murphey retreated to the Texas music scene, alongside Willie Nelson and Jerry Jeff Walker, playing country rock. A champion of Indian rights, Murphey penned 'Geronimo's Cadillac', one of the finest protest songs in popular music. In the seventies Murphey worked with producer Bob Johnston and released, 'Geronimo's Cadillac', 'Cosmic Cowboy Souvenir' and 'Michael Martin Murphey'. The next two albums, 'Swans Against The Sun' and 'Flowing Free Forever' gave Murphey crossover success but he was still something of an outsider and in 1979 he headed to New Mexico.

Blending country, rock, Spanish and Indian styles, he came up with another album titled 'Michael Martin Murphey' for Liberty and was finally embraced by country music when he won best new artist awards from the Academy Of Country Music and the Country Music Association. His videos also began to win awards and in 1985 his 'Tonight We Ride' album included three country chart singles.

But his biggest hits were to come on the 1987 album, 'Americana', notably his duet with Holly Dunn on 'A Long Line Of Love' which took the number one spot and was nominated for a Grammy for country duet of the year.

Times have come full circle with Murphey's 1988 album, 'River Of Time' with Murphey recording the 20-year-old song he first gave to The Monkees, 'What Am I Doin' Hangin' Round'. Murphey's career proves that country music will embrace those artists more concerned with their art and integrity than big bucks. Murphey, by remaining true to his visions, has enjoyed both and given his record company, Warner Bros, years of successful loyalty.

☆　★　★　★　☆

New Grass Revival

When four great musicians play together sparks fly and when those musicians, after years of struggling to find the right blend, hit upon the right formula, then country bands had better watch out. The members of New Grass Revival, Sam Bush, John Cowan, Pat Flynn and Bela Fleck, are among Nashville's finest and all earn vast sums as session players. But for all four their band is the prime commitment.

For years they've enjoyed an enviable reputation as one of the most dynamic live outfits in American music. Recently with the release of a 1988 album, 'Hold To A Dream' (EMI/Capitol), their recorded output has created renewed interest in modern-style bluegrass music.

Back in 1970 Sam Bush replaced Dan Crary as guitarist for bluegrass group, The Bluegrass Alliance. A gifted multi-instrumentalist, Bush had won the National Old Time Fiddlers Contest three years running. Unfortunately Crary took the band's name with him when he left so the remaining players, Courtney Johnson (banjo), Curtis Burch (guitar and dobro) and Ebo Walker (bass) came up with a new name, New Grass Revival. "At the time," remembers Bush, "we were basically your bluegrass kind of guys who were rockin' out on our instruments. That's really what newgrass is – contemporary music played with bluegrass-style instruments."

The band released an album in 1972 but in 1973 Ebo Walker left to be replaced by John Cowan who brought with him a naturally powerful singing voice. Cowan was a rock musician, a veteran of several Louisville rock bands, who had never played bluegrass before, and Bush realised that his addition gave the band both an edge and a lift. "Before John joined people just tolerated our vocals. With John we finally had a lead singer that could really grab the audience's attention."

Throughout the seventies the band released a number of well received small label albums and in 1979 raised their profile as opening act and back-up band for sometime country, sometime rock and blues artist Leon Russell. Russell's music is nothing if not diverse and the sheer musical ability of New Grass Revival allowed Russell to sweep through country, rock, blues, jazz and swing.

Exhausted by continual travelling in 1981 Curtis Burch and Courtney Johnson quit the band. Fortunately two replacements were immediately at hand, respected West Coast guitarist Pat Flynn and banjo prodigy Bela Fleck. With acoustic music making inroads into mainstream country music it seemed that New Grass Revival's day had come but it took the 1988 album, 'Hold To A Dream' (Capitol) to lift them into the top league. And it was about time. "Everybody we grew up playing with has now made it on their own, like Vince Gill, Ricky Skaggs, Bill Lloyd," says John Cowan. "Sometime's it's a little galling to see all your friends succeeding. It's sort of like, 'What's wrong with this picture'."

What was wrong until 'Hold To A Dream' was that New Grass Revival were almost too good, too creative and too diverse for their own good. "We never were pure country," said Fleck in 1988. "Sometimes it's as fast as a rock show and we also play jazz and blues, that kind of confused radio for a long time. I mean we're a new act as far as mainstream country is concerned, but the band has been together for years and we play around 200 shows a year and have a large body of support."

Drums were added for the 'Hold To A Dream' sessions and a more commercial outlook prevailed. Cowan feels it's their best album yet, but still the band aren't satisfied they've captured their live form as well as they might. Says Pat Flynn, "People who see us live always say our sound is more exciting than in the studio. So we try to record with as few overdubs as possible. But what would really be good is a live album. That's something we're thinking very seriously about."

Nitty Gritty Dirt Band

It was fitting that The Nitty Gritty Dirt Band's 1988 album, their most commercial in years, should be titled, 'Workin' Band' (Warners) for that's exactly what the band have been for more than 20 years. While they made a critically praised country album in 1973 with 'Will The Circle Be Unbroken?', it wasn't until recently that The Dirt Band launched itself into country music, but success has come rapidly.

Beginning in California in the mid-sixties as a jug band and then a country rock outfit (Jackson Browne was a short-term member) they settled on a hardcore line-up in the late sixties with founder member Jeff Hanna joined by Jimmy Fadden, Jimmy Ibbotson and John McEuen. Only recently did McEuen leave to be replaced by Bob Carpenter. The band's initial success came in the early seventies on Liberty Records with hit singles, 'Mr Bojangles', 'House At Pooh Corner' and Mike Nesmith's 'Some Of Shelly's Blues' but they slipped from view through the seventies and eighties.

Their finest country moments came in 1973 on the ambitious three-record set, 'Will The Circle Be Unbroken?' which saw them joined by old-time greats, Maybelle Carter, Earl Scruggs, Roy Acuff, Doc Watson, Merle Travis, Jimmy Martin, Vassar Clements and Norman Blake. Recorded live on a two-track machine, the results were quite amazing and marked an important point in the acceptance of long haired 'hippy' types by country music establishment figures. Unfortunately the band still didn't make inroads into the legitimate country music world.

Subsequent album releases were peppered with country-flavoured material but still The Dirt Band were seen as more of a rock band than a country outfit. Not even dropping the Nitty Gritty from their name could grab them a country audience. Because of their impressive history and outstanding live shows, the band were able to continue working even through the lean years and held out until country music again looked backwards to a sparser sound.

In 1983 the band moved from Liberty to Warners and gradually forced their way on to country radio with a slew of top 10 hits, 'High Horse', 'I Only Love You', 'Pardners Brothers And Friends', 'Soldier Of Love' and more. Their 1988 album, 'Workin' Band' consolidated their position as a *bona fide* country act. They give much of the credit to producer Josh Leo. "Josh looked into what we are live and was able to make that work on album, which is great since we're a real high energy band," says founder member Jeff Hanna.

The album blew hot with a barrage of country styles from the mandolin driven 'Soldier Of Love' to a Cajun beat on 'Johnny O'. For years the band had been trying to blend their musical interests into a cohesive whole. This album achieved just that. The next project, 'Will The Circle Be Unbroken II' should, in the present country climate, take The Nitty Gritty Dirt Band to the very top of the country music heap. In 1973 their delving into the folk side of country was considered oddball, now it's par for the course, except of course The Dirt Band do it better than most.

☆ ★ ★ ★ ☆

Mark O'Connor

Mark O'Connor has been one of country music's most sought after musicians for the past decade. A child prodigy in the seventies, O'Connor was compared to Doc Watson by *Guitar Player Magazine*. "He flatpicks bluegrass music in a clear, rippling style punctuated with unexpected chromatic flurries, effective syncopations and blues bends, and that's just the first cut." Considering he's also Nashville's top fiddle player it's apparent that O'Connor has played a key role in the development of new country. Besides being one of America's most respected sidemen, O'Connor has recorded a number of solo albums for independent labels including 'National Junior Fiddle Champion', 'Pickin' In The Wind', 'Markology', 'On The Rampage' and 'Soppin' The Gravy' all recorded on Rounder.

In 1979 David Grisman, world famous mandolin player, called on Mark O'Connor to play guitar on a tour with Stephane Grappelli. O'Connor learned his 20 or so numbers in just three days and won standing ovations for his playing on the tour.

In the eighties Mark played and recorded with the innovative Dixie Dregs, Chris Hillman, Peter Rowan and Doc Watson. Throughout, he was picking up awards left right and centre. *Esquire* magazine even listed him in a register of America's new leadership class as one of the outstanding men and women under 40 who were changing the nation. More down to earth was a 1983 move to Nashville where, after a blitz of recording sessions with top names, he signed a solo deal with Warner Bros and in 1986 released his début album, 'Meanings Of'.

The follow-up 'Stone From Which The Arch Was Made', showed amazing originality and saw O'Connor moving into a new age consciousness. His 1988 album, 'Elysian Forest' was a culmination, putting Mark O'Connor alongside new age artists like Andrea Wollenweider as a creator of musical depth, colour and imagination. His work mixes rock, jazz Celtic tunes, jazz and classical. Warners' Nashville bosses see no reason why O'Connor's instrumental work shouldn't move him into the gold record division.

The O'Kanes

Jamie O'Hara and Kieran Kane, collectively The O'Kanes, are the most promising and exciting male duo to emerge from Nashville since Phil and Don back in the fifties.

O'Hara, from Toledo, Ohio, was a high school All-American football half-back, but knee injuries forced him to end his sporting ambitions prematurely. "My father gave me a guitar as a gift. Two years later I was in Nashville. That either shows a lot of confidence, a lot of arrogance or a lot of stupidity."

Kane from Queens, New York lived the rock 'n' roll lifestyle, starting out as drummer in his brother's rock band at the age on nine. He developed an interest in country music but didn't feel confident that his brand of country would fit into the Nashville mainstream. Instead he went to LA and opened shows for The Steve Miller Band and Country Joe And The Fish. "I had wanted to move to Nashville before I went to LA but I didn't think what I was doing was country. I loved country music very much but I thought that what I was doing wouldn't be accepted by country music, and at that time – the early seventies – it wouldn't have been."

Both men concentrated on individual songwriting careers and had songs covered by Ronnie McDowell, The Judds, Southern Pacific, Tanya Tucker and others. But both felt they had reached a plateau in their music careers. "I think Kieran and I had become disenchanted with the way our lives within the industry were going. I think it was a question of maturity, both Kieran and I, totally independent of each other, reached a time when there were things we wanted to achieve and there were certain things we wanted to leave behind."

Nashville is a small town in music business terms and O'Hara and Kane developed a friendship based on mutual respect of each other's songwriting talents. Naturally they began collaborating on material, demoed the songs in Kane's attic studio and were eventually signed by CBS who released their self-titled début album, completely unchanged. The attic recordings became the album. They made the charts with their first single, 'Darlin'' and followed that with a number one, 'Can't Stop My Heart From Loving You'. The album won praise from the country and rock press. They received four nominations for Country Music Association awards, a Grammy nomination and *Billboard* awards for top new country group and top new country artists. They played a series of sell-out shows culminating in a reputation-building European visit in Spring 1988.

Their blend of Everlys and Louvins-inspired harmonies, West Coast song structures and bluegrass-style instrumentation lashed to a rock beat, was proving immensely popular. The album was low-key, a late night listening record, but their live shows were fast paced, rip-roaring affairs.

For their second album The O'Kanes opted to try and capture that live edge, not with a concert recording but by keeping the sound as live as possible in the studio. Unusually they recorded the album with their road band. O'Hara explained, "The stage became a sort of laboratory for us. We worked up songs during sound checks and tried them out, so we had what you might call laboratory results before we went into the studio to put it down." In the studio the O'Kanes avoided overdubs. "I think people feel that subliminally. They might not know what the difference is, but they know there's a difference."

The second album, 'Tired And Runnin'' (CBS) is a far more lively affair than their début offering. The songs continue to be first rate and the playing is impeccable, but The O'Kanes themselves sound far more committed, more fired up on their vocals.

Clearly one of the more adventurous and experimental acts in the new country vein, The O'Kanes have followed the likes of Skaggs and Yoakam in winning plaudits from the traditional country audience as well as younger rock fans. Their look is hip, the sound exciting and the future looks bright.

K.T. Oslin

K.T. Oslin has made a most dramatic and remarkable entry into country. She's in her mid-forties and shies away from rhinestones and cornball, "Forty-five is pretty late to make a comeback but I hadn't even started," she exclaims somewhat taken aback at her meteoric rise to win the Country Music Association's best female vocalist award and a Grammy in 1988, the same year as her début album made the highest entry into the country charts ever by a female artist.

Oslin has brought a maturity and wit to country music and also given a voice to older women everywhere. Moreover Kay Toinette Oslin is not a part of Nashville's artist community. "I don't listen to the radio, buy records or go to concerts. I like it that way. I don't hear the latest George Strait song on the radio and unconsciously write it all over again," she says. At one time, back in the sixties she positively despised country music . . . "When it was all middle aged men singing about drinking whiskey and cheating on their wives."

As a kid she fell for the music of Hank Williams, Hank Snow and The Carter Family. Her family moved from Mobile to Houston when she was a teenager. She embraced rock 'n' roll and was inspired by the Texas folk music boom. "My first gig was as a folk singer in a club in Houston in the early sixties." She played the circuits, even winding up in a folk group with Guy Clark. But folk music was confining for Oslin and she moved into musical theatre, eventually touring in *Hello Dolly* with Carol Channing. She was then chosen for the Broadway performance and moved to New York in 1967 aged 24. Sadly, stardom never beckoned and a string of small parts, including a haemorrhoids commercial proved far from satisfying.

She also worked as a jingles singer and was once selected for a Coca Cola campaign. "I was the Coca Cola cowgirl. And I got a cheque for $38," she recalls. But the experience whetted her appetite for songwriting and in the eighties she landed a deal with WEA who released a version of 'Younger Men', later to appear on her RCA début. This version flopped and the song was regarded as too 'women's lib'. "Radio people practically slapped me on the wrist because they thought the song would offend their male listeners." Oslin's contract was terminated. "I got real fat and depressed," she remembers. "I felt like everything was passing me by. I had to give it one more try." She borrowed $7000 from an aunt and hired a band for a Nashville showcase. People were impressed but thought Oslin was too old. KT was devastated. "Tell me I'm bad or I can't write but don't just go telling me I'm too old."

One man liked what he heard and saw. Top producer and now head of Polygram Nashville, Harold Shedd asked if he could record a couple of songs with her. He took the tapes to Joe Galante at RCA who was struck by Oslin's facility for lyric writing. RCA signed her, recorded the '80s Ladies' album and she was on her way. Her success with the début record is all the more impressive considering that some radio stations refused to play her because the songs were thought too feminist. Fortunately commonsense prevailed and Oslin broke through with a brand of lyrical and musical intelligence unheard of in Nashville since early Loretta Lynn.

Musically, Oslin is a diverse artist. "All kinds of styles have little flare ups in my music," she says. "There are forms of music that are indigenous to America – jazz, blues, American folk, country, rock 'n' roll – these are what we call our native American music. When I sit down to write, all of these things that I've listened to come together in my music." Oslin's voice, warm and pure, blends beautifully into a lush production on her albums.

Her début introduced Oslin's use of characters in songs and her tough optimistic lyrics. The controversial 'Younger Men' opens with . . . 'Women peak at 40, men at 19/ I remember laughing my head off when I read that in a magazine,' – hardly a traditional line for country music women.

Fortunately there were enough women and men to appreciate her insights and wit, and they thronged to Oslin's concerts and eagerly awaited the release of her follow-up 1988 album, 'This Woman'. Oslin has no intention of compromising her lyrics to reach a mass audience. "I try to make the women in my songs as strong as possible. I don't want them to be wimps or victims." The sound on 'This Woman' was much in the same vein as the first RCA album but the lyrics sounded more confident, even more witty and sassy.

Only a performer completely at ease with themselves could produce lyrics like, 'I'm overworked and overweight/I can't remember when I last had a date/ Oh I didn't expect it to go down this way,' and 'Been dating for years, honey that ain't natural/ I thought by now I'd find my man and settle down/ Ain't a good one left in town.' These days Oslin dates top producer Steve Buckingham who has likened her music to a cross between Kitty Wells and Aretha Franklin. In time KT Oslin could outdo both of those legendary female artists.

☆ ★ ★ ★ ☆

Restless Heart

Since their inception in 1985, Restless Heart have injected a pop sensibility into new country music. In April 1987 they hit the top five of the *Billboard* Adult Contemporary chart with 'I'll Still Be Loving You', the first time in more than three years that a Nashville country act had managed that feat, and it was country music's biggest crossover success since Kenny Rogers and Dolly Parton scored with 'Islands In The Stream'.

Restless Heart consists of Larry Stewart, Greg Jennings, Dave Innis, Paul Gregg and John Dittrich, who work very closely with co-producers Scott Hendricks and Tim DuBois. But things didn't always look rosy for the band. In an article in *Pulse* magazine in 1986 Innis remembered a crisis point. "We didn't have a record deal and Tim was paying for us out of his savings account. We decided that instead of doing something that we thought we could get a deal on, let's do something we believe in. Let's have fun and make the kind of music we want to make, so if we get a deal we can really hold our heads high and be proud and continue to play the songs for years to come."

The band relaxed and discovered a new style, strong country roots laced with a West Coast pop flavour. Their début for RCA wasn't long coming and the eponymously titled album established their musical identity and proved a springboard for the very successful follow-up LP, 'Wheels' (RCA) which featured no fewer than four number one singles, three of which also made it into the top 10 of the adult contemporary chart.

Clearly Restless Heart had carved themselves a niche as a latter-day Eagles, with soft rock, harmony-dominated country which proved just as popular with country radio as it did with the FM stations. Guitarist and vocalist Greg Jennings believes that the band tapped into a new market. "A new age of country listeners – people who grew up listening to both country and rock music in the sixties and seventies. It's this sort of hybrid of listener that our music particularly appeals to, because it's got country harmonies but a sort of rock edge to it as well."

The band toured extensively after the success of 'Wheels' in 1987, opening for Alabama, Randy Travis and Hank Williams as well as AOR rockers Bruce Hornsby And The Range. They were also nominated for Grammy, Country Music Association and Academy Of Country Music awards. Live, Restless Heart are slick without being glitzy, tight without being over-rehearsed. Their music may be highly polished and far more textured than many of their country rivals but every single band member plays and sings with intensity and conviction.

Restless Heart may play a West Coast inspired, laid-back sound but their performances are rarely boring. As singer Larry Stewart explained after a Randy Travis concert . . . "Those people who went crazy for Randy Travis also went crazy for Restless Heart. And you can't get two more opposite ends of the country spectrum than that. I think it just proves that people appreciate good music, and can sense the warmth and sincerity that comes through when the people on-stage really mean what they're singing."

Their 1988 album saw the band progressing with more musical sidesteps and lyrical manoeuvres. Says Stewart, "We took a different approach. What you hear is still Restless Heart but our individual personalities have become much more incorporated into the overall sound." More diverse certainly but also a tougher, leaner sound obviously honed on the road over the months.

There's more of a live feel to 'Big Dreams In A Small Town' (RCA) with vocals recorded live rather than overdubbing layers of voices. The material on the third album certainly matched up to 'Wheels' with Don Schlitz contributing 'Say What's In Your Heart' and band members co-writing the toe-tapping rocker 'El Dorado' and the almost funky 'This Time'. Restless Heart have proved that soft country need not mean boring country.

Judy Rodman

The careers of Judy Rodman and her label MTM have dovetailed to mutual advantage. MTM gave Rodman her chance and she repaid the company by giving them their first number one single. She's now one of Nashville's brightest stars.

Born in California, Rodman travelled extensively as a child living in England, Mississippi, Tennessee, Alaska and Florida where she studied music at Jacksonville University. Her family were all musical and from the age of four Rodman accompanied her father on dates. "We'd sing in old folks' homes, in cars and for relatives in Mississippi," she recalls.

Her professional career began when she was 17 and started singing on jingles. In 1971 her family moved to Memphis where Judy found work singing jingles for the Tanner Agency, doing sessions for demos and playing with local band, Phase II. In Memphis she befriended another would-be star, Janie Fricke, married John Rodman and became a mother with the birth of son Peter.

In 1980 the Rodmans moved to Nashville and worked on jingles for Kelloggs, McDonalds, Budweiser and a host of other major companies. As a harmony singer she worked behind Crystal Gale, George Jones, Dolly Parton and Merle Haggard. Producer Tommy West liked the sound of Rodman's voice and when he was eventually named Senior Director of A&R at MTM, Rodman was his first signing. Her first album, 'Judy', was also MTM's first album release and a year later, 'Until I Met You' became Rodman's and MTM's first number one single.

After years singing to specific directions Rodman was finally a successful solo artist, not just a voice. She told *The Tennesseean*, "I love it. It allows me to be myself. After you've been singing for years and blending in with other voices, you wonder if you can be yourself." Rodman took a while to adjust to the rigours of touring and promoting her records and her second album, 'A Place Called Love', wasn't released until 1987.

One song, Bob Dylan's 'I'll Be Your Baby Tonight', relates directly to the *Farm Aid* concert in 1985. A van drove past Rodman in the parking lot, a window opened and a voice told Rodman that he loved her music. Rodman didn't realise it, but the admirer was none other than Dylan himself who later wrote on his 'Biograph' sleeve notes, "At the moment I like Judy Rodman's 'I've Been Had By Love Before' more than anything happening on the pop stations." Hence the compliment was repaid with Rodman recording a Dylan tune.

Rodman's 1988 album, 'Goin' To Work', again proved her abilities and her video for the title track was one of the most dynamic of the year.

☆ ★ ★ ☆

Schuyler Knobloch And Bickhardt

Perhaps the most unusual name in country music, Schuyler, Knobloch and Bickhardt, also known simply as SKB, have brought a much needed levity to Nashville country music. In a music scene dominated by the search for hit records, pressure to succeed can render some artists po-faced and self important. Not so SKB. While never allowing it to detract from their musical abilities, their shows follow in the great tradition of humour and entertainment in country. Fred Knobloch in particular is a natural communicator, a character on and off stage. Add to this a long resumé of writing credits and musical talent and SKB have much going for them.

Thom Schuyler from Bethlehem, Pennsylvania, a carpenter by trade, moved to Nashville in 1978. His carpentry work found him employed by Jim Malloy and Eddie Rabbitt re-modelling their studio. Thom had already written several songs and Rabbitt and Molloy liked what they heard. He signed with their publishing company and there he remained until 1983 when he signed a solo deal with Capitol Records who released an album, 'Brave Heart' from which he scored two top 30 singles.

Fred Knobloch (pronounced no-block) hails from Jackson, Mississippi. A wit and raconteur, he attended Louisiana State University majoring in journalism and creative writing. Meanwhile his skills as a musician found him plenty of work in the recording studios of Atlanta and Los Angeles. He moved to Nashville in 1983, the same year as Schuyler.

Craig Bickhardt replaced original member Paul Overstreet who left to pursue other directions. From Pennsylvania, Bickhardt and his band Wire And Wood, had opened shows for Springsteen, Stephen Stills and Harry Chapin before leaving Philadelphia for LA in 1974. They moved back to the east however, shortly after fire destroyed their home. His next band, The Craig Bickhardt Band, won quite a following and opened for Steve Forbert, Little Feat, Dr John and The Hooters. He also signed a writing deal with Screen Gems/EMI in New York and wrote Randy Meisner's top 40 hit 'Never Been In Love'. Bickhardt was later asked to work in Nashville recording two songs for the Robert Duvall country music tinged movie *Tender Mercies*. Soon after he moved to Nashville and met up with Knobloch and Schuyler.

SKB have a début album on MTM awaiting release but in the meantime have been busy on the road. Unlike many bands, SKB have one distinct advantage – all three members are prolific writers. Schuyler has written hits for Eddie Rabbitt, Kenny Rogers, Crystal Gale and others. Knobloch has versions from Ray Charles, Marie Osmond, The Dirt Band and The Everlys to his credit and Bickhardt has written for Art Garfunkel, BB King and The Judds. Their only problem is choosing which of their songs to keep for SKB.

Dan Seals

There's a quiet dignity about Dan Seals and his music. His country is of the gentle kind, more Don Williams than Dwight Yoakam and in his own field he is a master. Seals started out as one half of a pop act, England Dan and John Ford Coley, but devoted himself to a country career in the eighties.

He got off to an inauspicious start for in 1982 he was bankrupt and his early releases on EMI/Capitol in 1983 fared only reasonably well. The following year however, he conjured up a string of top 10 hits, notably 'My Baby's Got Good Timin'' and 'Old Yellow Car'. In 1985 he hit the top spot with 'Meet Me In Montana' a duet with Marie Osmond which also earned an award from the Country Music Association. In 1986 his single 'Bop' was named as the Country Music Association's single of the year, and his 1987 album, 'Won't Be Blue Anymore', went gold soon after release.

It would appear that Seals did the right thing by leaving pop for country. His 1988 album saw him crossing more barriers. More traditional-sounding than previous albums the record was immaculately produced and featured some remarkably insightful lyrics. Half the songs on the album are Seals' originals and they're probably the best of the bunch, although new writers Bob McDill and John Scott Sherrill make some moving contributions on the album.

Seals has much to say. "I don't hear enough social comment songs and sometimes the world is in dire need of them." He is a gentle and spiritual man. "I sometimes wish I was eloquent and could sum up what I like, what I'm worried about and what I want for people. But when I get away from music I almost get tongue-tied."

Unlike some of his country cohorts Seals has placed his career in context. Several years ago he made a profoundly moving trip to India. "I think that anyone who thinks they're real good should take a trip to India as I did, and see people starving to death. That was a double dose of reality. It broke my heart so I don't worry too much about how I'm dressed and who I'm seen with. We live in such a naïve world in the United States and country music." Not surprising perhaps that his 1988 album should be titled 'Rage On' (EMI).

Shenandoah

There's a strong soul edge to the music of new CBS band, Shenandoah. With five renowned musicians and a core of original material, Shenandoah have produced a fine début, 'Shenandoah' for CBS. The gritty sound, a shade more Memphis than Nashville, again proved how diverse country music has become through the eighties. Far removed from the styles of The Judds and Dwight Yoakam, it somehow shares a common freshness and vitality.

Marty Raybon, lead vocalist, grew up in Florida, a bluegrass fanatic and for many years a songwriter and session player in Nashville. Mike McGuire, a hard-hitting drummer, settled in Muscle Shoals and found success as a songwriter (T. Graham Brown had a hit with his 'She Couldn't Love Me Anymore'). Bass player Ralph Ezell was a session player at Fame Studios in Muscle Shoals and has played on numerous albums, the most interesting perhaps being Bill Haley's last recordings. Lead guitarist Jimmy Seales avoided a musical career until later in life. His early ambition was to teach English in school but he found singing and playing more rewarding intellectually and financially. Session work in Muscle Shoals followed. Keyboard player Stan Thorn grew up smitten by the joys of gospel music and played music full-time after dropping out of college. At one point in the seventies he was a member of Funkadelic.

Local producers Rick Hall and Robert Byrne discovered the band just a mile down the road from their offices playing in the nearby clubs and bars, and gracing numerous sessions as individuals. Byrne approached CBS for a singles deal and took them seven songs. CBS liked them all and signed Shenandoah to an album contract.

The power of their 1989 album, 'The Road Not Taken!' recorded at the Fame studios in Muscle Shoals, proves that this band will be at the fore of new country for some time to come.

BELOW: RICKY SCAGGS WITH PRINCESS ANNE
OPPOSITE: WITH ELVIS COSTELLO

Ricky Skaggs

Without the pioneering work of Ricky Skaggs there probably wouldn't be any new country or new traditionalist music. It was Skaggs' vision and ability to make old-time acoustic music commercial and popular that broke the country pop stranglehold on Nashville's output. In the mid-eighties his ground breaking work was rewarded with a collection of gold albums and industry awards. Recently his thunder has been stolen by the amazing success of Randy Travis, but his music continues to amaze and move and it won't be long before Skaggs again tops the pile.

Born in 1954 near Cordell in Kentucky, Ricky grew up in an old fashioned, family based environment. Religion and music were major factors in his early life and it was music that took Skaggs to prominence. At the age of just seven he appeared on TV with Flatt and Scruggs. By 15 he was playing with The Ralph Stanley Band alongside Keith Whitley, another young player who would later find solo success in country music. Bluegrass festival audiences were deeply impressed by the youngsters' playing and singing and they became bluegrass celebrities while still teenagers.

Skaggs married one of Stanley's cousins and moved to Manassas to work for an electric company, but at weekends he still played music. After a while he was asked to play fiddle with the Country Gentlemen, a move that allowed him to devote all his energies to a career in country music. His high harmonies, multi-instrumental skills and stage presence marked Skaggs as a potential star. He was also ambitious and formed his own band Boone Creek who recorded two high quality albums. In 1977 Rodney Crowell left Emmylou Harris' Hot Band and Skaggs was recruited to cover guitar, fiddle, mandolin and high harmony duties. As it turned out he played a key role in directing Harris into the old-time sounds and Skaggs played a key role on her acoustic masterpiece 'Roses In The Snow' which won a Grammy.

In 1980 Skaggs embarked on a solo career with independent label Sugar Hill, calling on music industry friends to help out on his solo album 'Sweet Temptations' (Sugar Hill). Albert Lee, Emmylou, Jerry Douglas and Bobby Hicks all played on what became one of the best received acoustic albums of the eighties. His attempt to

drag bluegrass music out of a ghetto was beginning to work. "You see people are kind of prejudiced against bluegrass because of the real high singing but when people give it a chance, especially the younger bands, they see that the energy and drive is very close to rock 'n' roll."

Slowly Skaggs was proving his point. Thanks to the critical reception granted to 'Sweet Temptations' and his work behind the scenes with Emmylou, Skaggs was given a contract by Epic Records. He débuted in the country charts with an update of the old Flatt And Scruggs number, 'Don't Get Above Your Raising'. The following album, 'Waiting For The Sun To Shine' saw his new style dominating the 1982 country radio airwaves. Two singles from the album made number one, 'Crying My Heart Out Over You' and 'I Don't Care' and he was rewarded with the Country Music Association's award for best male vocalist.

In the light of the new traditionalist movement his achievement may not appear so great, but at the time, before George Strait was popular, before Reba McEntire was a superstar, before The Judds captured hearts with their mountain harmonies, Skaggs was breaking through country music's lowest ebb. The late seventies and early eighties had seen country go pop. "It was a depressing period for those of us who love the old-time sounds, banjos and fiddles and stuff because it was all strings or synthesizers. Country music had lost sight of its roots." But Skaggs re-introduced the backwoods sound and with an impeccably tight band and clear, snappy bluegrass-influenced productions, his records and live shows came like a breath of fresh air through a stagnant Nashville smog.

Skaggs, a southern gent, is humble about his role in new country music. "There were other artists doing what we were doing but I guess we were the ones who broke through first." And break through they did. His version of Bill Monroe's 'Uncle Pen' was the first bluegrass tune recorded by a solo artist to hit number one in the *Billboard* country chart since 1949. Skaggs also pioneered the development of new country into the European market. His 'Live In London' album recorded in 1985, including a guest appearance from Elvis Costello, won him support in the rock press and opened minds and doors for the eventual acceptance and popularity in Britain of Yoakam, Steve Earle, Nanci Griffith and Randy Travis.

Skaggs' 1987 album, 'Love's Gonna Get Ya' was a shade too slick for his own good but the follow-up, 'Comin' Home To Stay' was back to basic perfection. His duet with wife Sharon (he married Sharon White of The Whites in the eighties) on 'Home Is Wherever You Are' is back to 'Waitin' For The Sun To Shine' form. The writer, Wayland Patton, one of Skaggs' staff writers, first performed this at his wedding. Ricky was deeply moved and wanted to cut it with Sharon. "Sharon's my duet partner in life and I think that a song like this by a husband and wife has more grit than if it was just two people who didn't have some kind of emotional bond."

Elsewhere the album typified Skaggs' sound – tight, high harmonies, wicked instrumental twists and turns, songs with meat and a crystal clear production. As a producer Skaggs has learned fast. His own sound is always pure and free from cliché and in the autumn of 1988 he began work producing a back-to-basics album for Dolly Parton. "I guess she liked the sound I get but I think she also needed a strong personality who wouldn't be afraid to tell her if she was wrong. And I sure don't mind telling people what I think."

Still in his mid-thirties, Skaggs is something of a music business veteran. He handles his own affairs, organises his own bookings and runs not just a band but a publishing company to boot. Just like Chet Atkins in the sixties Skaggs could become one of the key figures in country music's development in the nineties.

Darden Smith

Darden Smith is another Texas songwriter to emerge in the new country movement. Younger than his friends and allies Lyle Lovett and Nanci Griffith, he shares their predilection for quality lyrics and heart-tugging melodies.

Named after a renowned local rodeo star, Darden was raised on a farm in Brenham, Texas. Inspired by the breadth of musical styles he heard on street corners and radio stations, Smith began writing songs before he was 10-years-old. A couple of years into high school Smith's family moved to Houston where the eager lad was immediately drawn to a bubbling music scene. He could barely wait to start playing and soon connived his way into his older brother's band. "See his band needed a microphone and I'd saved some money, so I bought one and offered it to them. Then I told them, 'Oh yeah I come with the mike!' They went for it even though they didn't play for a year."

Smith continued playing, singing and writing until he started college in San Marcos. But he soon realised that Austin was a hotbed of progressive music. "I really started liking what was happening in Texas in the late seventies. And I'd also been a big fan of The Allman Brothers and Marshall Tucker. Plus I got into Bob Dylan when I was 16. I started thinking of different ways of saying things."

Smith tied his own musical interests and influence to the country styles of Austin and found himself in demand in the local club scene. "I could play maybe three times a week, making $20 a night. I thought I was making big bucks." Something of a celebrity on the local scene Smith decided to record his own album. "But I didn't think I'd grown up enough so I decided to wait until I got out of college."

Smith graduated from the University of Texas in Austin with a degree in American Studies and put out an album, 'Native Soil' on his own Red Mix label. The album was low-key but literate and thoughtful and Smith showed that he understood song structures and the importance of producing quality material, even on a budget priced recording. "I wanted to make a record that would stand up to the years. Making sure everything was right really had a lot to do with me signing with CBS/Epic. I was 100 per cent committed to making a career in country music, I believe you have to be or you will never get anywhere. I hope that motivation and dedication come through. I hope people hear that in my music. "

CBS certainly heard potential in Darden Smith's self-made album and didn't waste time in signing him to the Epic label. His début album, 'Darden Smith', produced by Ray Benson of Asleep At The Wheel, is a country singer songwriter's album. He's certainly more country than Lyle Lovett and Nanci Griffith who both pop up on his album, but he shares their vision of Texas and ability to create enchanting tales and scenarios.

The variety of Texas sounds Smith grew up with in Houston are given vent together with a Cajun Louisiana feel provided by Sonny Landreth and CJ Chenier, and some nods in the direction of swing King Bob Wills in various places. There's a rich, soulful bluesy timbre to Smith's voice and more so than most Texas writers he frequently looks outward to the wider world of LA in 'Place In Time' and New England on 'Coldest Winter'. He's also capable of spine tingling melodies as the ballad 'Little Maggie' adequately proves. There's no swagger with Smith, no hip haircuts, no affectations, just down to earth intelligent observations, notions and melodies.

Russell Smith

Although regarded as a new artist, husky voiced Russell Smith first surfaced in the mid-seventies with respected Memphis country rockers The Amazing Rhythm Aces. Fusion was the name of their game, country and blues, rock and soul. Their sound was tough, dynamic and progressive as their début album 'Stacked Deck' proved. However the band failed to take off commercially and disbanded in 1980.

Russell Smith, The Aces' lead vocalist embarked upon a semi-successful solo career with Capitol, releasing a fine album, 'The Boy Next Door'. But this was a shade before dusty, back-to-basics, rock tinged country was in vogue. Once it was, Smith was chased by Epic and given the chance to make his own kind of music. It suits him better than being part of a band. "Now I'm the boss, I get to hire who I want, it's all my show," he says.

His Epic début in 1988, 'This Little Town' saw Smith co-writing every song on the album and creating a hard-edged free-flowing country rock sound. "I think it's a good time for me. The way I see it, there's a place for me right between Steve Earle and T. Graham Brown, that's what I'm shooting for."

Jo-El Sonnier

Like many of the emerging country artists Jo-El Sonnier paid his dues with a series of small label albums and years of touring before reaching the attention of a major league record company. As country music re-discovers its roots, Sonnier's brew of rock flavoured Cajun music is perfectly placed to break both Sonnier and Cajun out of the swamp ghetto.

With roots music of all descriptions re-surfacing and progressing with the aid of contemporary technology, it was just a matter of time before record companies realised the quality, passion and drive of Louisiana boogie and nobody could have capitalized better than Jo-El Sonnier. Sonnier, at home with both ethnic and rock styles, is a master of his own region's music and has progressed through a rock and country learning process to become one of the best respected accordion players in America. Like Robert Cray in the blues field, Sonnier is skilled, articulate and intelligent enough to take an ethnic style into the mainstream without diluting the qualities that first made the music so vital.

Born in Rayne, a rural area of Louisiana, in 1946 to sharecropper parents, Sonnier toiled hard as he grew up. But meantime he was rapidly learning the accordion and at just six-years-old he had his own 15-minute radio slot in nearby Crowley. "I had to get up at four, milk the cows, feed the pigs and pick one row of cotton and then Dad would drive me to the station," he remembers.

At 13 he made his first recording, 'Tes Yeux Bleus' (Your Blue Eyes) and went on to record for small local labels Swallow and Goldblend as well as gigging every weekend. "I met a lot of legends – Sidney Brown, Iry LeJeune, Shorty LeBlanc and I feel their presence around me still today when I perform. The way music was back then, people would work hard all week long, and then on weekends they'd still play their music. It always made me feel good. Some of the songs had to be played real deep. I've worked to capture that French blues sound, that crying style."

By 26 Sonnier was a local legend and decided to spread his wings and give California a try. His French accent was still very strong at the time and sometimes he needed an interpreter. Work was sporadic and he made most of his money gigging as an accordion player in the bars and honky-tonks of the south-west. In the mid-seventies he returned to the south, this time to Tennessee and Nashville where he spent six years building a sizeable reputation as a songwriter and musician. He recorded for Mercury and had songs covered by George Strait and Johnny Cash. In 1980 he returned to Louisiana and cut the seminal Cajun album, 'Cajun Live' (Rounder). Still not finding his music accepted, Sonnier went back to California and toured with some musician friends, among them Albert Lee, David Lindley and Garth Hudson. Elvis Costello saw his show and, completely blown over, recruited Sonnier for his 'King Of America' album. But still no bite from a major record company.

Sonnier stepped into a routine of commuting between Nashville and his wife Jami's home in Louisiana. "I was starting to give up hope of ever making it. All the years of knocks and frustrations were beginning to take their toll. But then things clicked with Joe Galante and RCA. He brought the entire staff down to hear me at a little club in Sunset, Louisiana, and soon afterwards we signed a contract." Galante understood the special nature of Sonnier's appeal. The roots and rough edges were part of Jo-El's attraction and with polish he could appeal to a far wider audience. Top songs were picked and Richard Bennett (Steve Earle) was brought in to produce.

A live feel was forged on the disc thanks to comprehensive pre-production. Says Bennett, "Once we were in the studio we never needed more than three or four takes on any song." The album, 'Come On Joe' complete with top-flight playing and crafty song selection is the perfect Cajun country album. Not too ethnic for mainstream fans but rootsy enough to interest rock and traditional ears. Stand out track has to be a Dave Edmunds-like version of Richard Thompson's blistering 'Tear Stained Letter'. Elsewhere Jo-El Sonnier dabbles with fast paced rock, edgy blues swamp boogie and down-home country. It's a testimony to the man's talent and experience that he can make each style sound his own.

Southern Pacific

Country rock lives with Southern Pacific. Reminiscent at times of early Eagles, this supergroup (the individual players are well known in their own right) play tough, with all the energy of a blaring rock band but also free gliding and as poetic and graceful as any of the early seventies country rock bands.

Southern Pacific débuted on vinyl in 1985 with a self-titled album for Warner Bros. Previous to that there had been an assembly of talents that hinged around the core

of ex-Doobie Brothers Keith Knudsen and John McFee. After nine years with
The Doobies, Knudsen worked with Nicolette Larson, Carly Simon and Emmylou
Harris. McFee spent the post-Doobie years experimenting with the cross-fertilisation
of country and rock with North Californian band Clover, who backed Elvis Costello on
his début country album 'My Aim Is True'.

   McFee and Knudsen began appearing on the same sessions and learned to respect
each other's work, demos they made together found their way to Jim Ed Norman
at Warners who immediately signed the pair. The next step was to recruit a band.
McFee contacted former Creedence Clearwater Revival bass player Stu Cook who
liked what he heard and signed on the dotted line. Keyboard player Kurt Howell came
to Southern Pacific via work with Waylon Jennings and Crystal Gale. Singer and
guitarist David Jenkins was an old friend of McFee's and a former member of Pablo
Cruise. He also sang back-up vocals on the Huey Lewis album, 'Fore'.

Very often the notion of a supergroup fails before it gets into the studio. Egos and personalities gel very rarely and fortunately for Southern Pacific this was one of those rare occasions. Their sound developed fast and the début album yielded two hit singles, 'Reno Bound' and 'Thing About You'. They were also hailed as Top New Country Act by *Billboard* in 1985. Extensive touring followed until album number two, 'Killbilly Hill'. The hits continued to flow including 'A Girl Like Emmylou' and 'Don't Let Go Of My Heart'. On the following tour the band's reputation grew rapidly and they were invited to play as far afield as Turkey, although the European tour was cut short following the American bombing of Libya.

McFee and Knudsen later teamed up with their old Doobie Brothers bandmates and conveniently Southern Pacific opened for some of their shows. In March 1987 the band began recording their third album but such was the demand for live work that it took almost a year to begin working solidly on the project.

McFee is convinced that recording after a hard tour was beneficial to their music. "Going out on the road and then coming back to the studio whenever we had the time was really a way for us to bring what we were doing together on-stage into a recording environment. The music evolved in some unique ways and I think that blend of country and rock became even more our own. We initially cut 10 tracks, but as we toured we kept writing and bringing the new stuff to the studio which gave us a lot of material to choose from.

Produced by Jim Ed Norman, 'Zuma' was a high point in Southern Pacific's short career: country combines with rock, losing nothing in the process, just gaining power and excitement sometimes lacking from traditional country bands.

GARY STEWART

Gary Stewart

Honky tonk singer songwriter Gary Stewart has been on the scene for many years flitting in and out of the public eye. He had a string of chart singles in the mid-seventies for RCA, made several excellent albums but found only limited radio exposure. Still well known as a writer, he teamed up in 1982 with new wild kid in town Dean Dillon and recorded an album, 'Brotherly Love' for RCA. Sadly the public and radio stations were not receptive.

Since then Stewart has continued his writing career and recently began recording again for independent label Hightone. His music has always been progressive and if he can harness his undeniable talents to a commercial ethos he could join the likes of Lyle Lovett and Dwight Yoakam at the drop of his stetson.

George Strait

Strait is the phenomenon of new country. Playing an essentially old fashioned honky tonk style, his albums enter the charts at number one and his shows sell out in hours. His quiet nature and liking for privacy have created a web of mystery around the biggest selling country act in America. His clean-cut, all-American image and the steel and fiddle dominated records have captured the imagination of the public throughout the eighties, however the extent of his popularity could never have been predicted.

Raised on a ranch in Texas, Strait dropped out of college to elope with his childhood sweetheart Norma, before joining the army where he gained his first real exposure as a singer with a country band in Hawaii, singing the songs of his idols – Merle Haggard, Bob Wills and Hank Williams. He returned to Texas after the army, attended college and majored in agriculture. But after his musical experiences in the army he couldn't devote himself totally to farming.

He put together a honky tonk group, The Ace In The Hole Band and picked up club work around Texas. "When you're a local act, and you're doing Merle Haggard and George Jones songs, people want you to sound like the records. So that's what you do; you sing like Merle or George and pretty soon that's just the way you sing. That's your style."

Strait and his band picked up regular work in Texas and caught the eye of former MCA promotions man Erv Woolsey. Woolsey won him a deal with MCA and became

Strait's manager, and in the process a very rich man. "Erv really helped me get my foot in the door at MCA. I don't know how many people heard my audition tape but Erv was instrumental in getting me signed there." MCA signed Strait early in 1981 and the first single made the top 10 of the country charts. From there it was success all the way as his albums went gold and singles topped the charts (he's on his sixteenth number one at the time of writing).

His albums, 'Strait Country', 'Something Special', 'Greatest Hits', 'Strait From The Heart', 'Does Fort Worth Ever Cross Your Mind', 'Number Seven, 'Ocean Front Property', 'If You Ain't Lovin', You Ain't Livin' – all on MCA – are classic country records. When the history of modern country music is written Strait's albums will rank alongside Haggard, Patsy Cline and George Jones. His voice is pure old-time country, the band, rough and rural but as good as any hand picked Nashville session band, and Strait himself may just be the finest country music performer since Hank Williams.

The albums are good, but Strait is at his best on-stage. Impeccably turned out (a critic once coined the phrase yuppie-billy just for George) and bashful but confident in front of the audience, Strait has been responsible for some of the wildest screaming from female country fans since Elvis Presley shook a hip or two. Live, Strait eschews the jazzier swing side of his recorded repertoire and concentrates on honky tonk. He sings old songs, new songs and some of the finest tear-jerkers since old Hank passed away.

Strait is a cagey character. As far as he's concerned his opinions are his and his alone. His records, by selling in such vast quantities, have set him apart from the rest of the country music fraternity but his success has also paved the way for other traditional sounding artists. First Skaggs and then Strait with a different kind of old-time country, proved that country roots were still preferable, even in the age of the compact disc.

Strait is a proud, upright Texan who works his farm when he's not on the road. He seems too good to be true at first glance but in truth Strait is exactly what he appears – honest, straight as an arrow and a man with a musical Midas touch. Every record he makes turns gold.

Sweethearts Of The Rodeo

One of the most progressive of Nashville's new acts, Janis Gill and Kristine Arnold, otherwise known as The Sweethearts Of The Rodeo, were the surprise find of 1987. Their cascading harmonies and tight country rock instrumentation swept hard and clear across country airwaves quickly putting the duo at the head of the Nashville newcomer league.

Janis and Kristine Oliver grew up in California and spent as much time singing as they did on the beach. Importantly they always sang together, honing that understanding that only brother or sister duos can foster. There was a burgeoning country rock scene in California as Kristine and Janis carved their musical style. They took their name after seeing The Byrds' 'Sweetheart Of The Rodeo' cowgal album cover in a record store. Kristine remembers that it was . . . "the look that really interested us. It was real colourful and old fashioned but it was also real hip, and that's what we wanted to be."

The girls listened to Dylan, The Beatles, Crosby, Stills, Nash And Young, The Eagles, Emmylou Harris. Nothing very surprising in that but they also started picking up tapes of Hank Williams and Buck Owens, old-timers considered un-cool by many but Kristine was taken by the sound. "It was so real, so heartfelt. And because it was kind of off-the-wall to be into Hank Williams when we were teenagers it was kind of hip in a way." And so they put together an act, country rock influenced but with strong country roots. They played shopping malls, pizza parlours and honky tonks. Emmylou Harris saw their act and invited the duo to sit in on one of her gigs. "We got to sing with the original Hot Band," they remember with pride.

But while they were improving as artists, and Janis was writing classy material, The Sweethearts were far from making it. "We just concentrated on our families. We both got married and kind of forgot about the music for a while and Janis moved to Nashville with her husband Vince Gill. Then one day she calls me up and says Nashville is really buzzing and I should move down, she thought we had a chance of making it this time."

And make it they did. The duo won the Wrangler country showdown. "Winning was nice and the money helped but it wasn't the same as getting a record deal, although I guess the publicity didn't do us any harm," says Kristine. Finally a showcase gig at the Bluebird whetted the appetites of CBS sufficiently to get The Sweethearts a singles deal. Once CBS realised the strength and potential of their act an album was released, self-titled of course like most country débuts. Unlike most however, this album yielded five hit singles.

Touring followed, something which Janis found difficult since her husband Vince was also on the road for long spells. "She had a few problems, they'd never see each other. It was different for me though because my husband is the tour manager so he's there with us all the time," says Kristine.

A second album, 'One Time One Night' saw an improvement in song quality. Janis Gill had come on leaps and bounds as a writer and her and Don Schlitz's 'Satisfy You' was picked as the album's first single. The album's title tune came from Los Lobos. With this and a Beatles cover version ('I Feel Fine'), the women had moved into a more contemporary sound but still it sounded hard country. The Los Lobos song in particular showed that Sweethearts Of The Rodeo understood as much about country rock as any in Nashville. Produced by Steve Buckingham the album reverberates with swirling harmonies, staccato electric guitar and a driving rhythm section. But at no time is beauty lost in the search for power.

Combining energy and grace, the album, and their live shows, were highlights of 1987 and 1988, winning fans in Europe and America from both the traditional country area and from rock fans. The Sweethearts Of The Rodeo also brought a sense of enthusiasm and style to new country and proved that sometimes, even if it takes 15 years, talent does win in the end.

OPPOSITE:
SISTERS JANIS GILL
(LEFT) AND KRISTINE
ARNOLD OF THE
SWEETHEARTS OF
THE RODEO

Marty Stuart

Stuart's roots lie in acoustic music but his recent recordings have been in the country rock vein. His roots shine through – clear vocals, strong melody lines and uncluttered production. With a rock approach and an acoustic spirit, Stuart could yet be the new country star to break into the pop charts.

As a kid in Mississippi, Stuart thrilled to soulful black rhythm and blues. At home he liked nothing more than to hear his Grandpa drag his bow across the fiddle strings. He had to learn how to play and by the age of 12 was on the road with Lester Flatt and The Nashville Grass. When Flatt died, Stuart played with Johnny Cash and Bob Dylan. In 1982 he recorded a solo album for Sugar Hill, 'Busy Bee Café'. CBS tried out the gifted player in 1986 but the album didn't catapult Stuart to stardom. He may have to wait for that.

In the meantime he's an avid collector of country music pictures and priceless guitars. He understands the history of country music and wants to play a role in its development. "Some things are meant to be – you just can't stop 'em. I've always known that someday I would be emphasising my own performance, so I took my time and enjoyed playing with and learning from other people."

☆ ★ ★ ★ ☆

Eric Taylor

Texas country/folk singer and songwriter Eric Taylor has played a key role in the development of many new country acts. At one time he was married to Nanci Griffith and was important in pushing her career forwards, and Lyle Lovett cites him as a great influence musically. Like Griffith and Lovett, Taylor has built himself a niche as an intelligent lyricist interested in losers and victims, and with a special interest in American Indians his songs are never commonplace.

He recorded an excellent album, 'Shameless Love', on his own Featherbed label but this was in the late seventies and no major labels were interested. In many ways Taylor was a decade ahead of his time. In recent years he's spent time working with narcotics abusers. Nanci Griffith recorded a Taylor song on her 'One Fair Summer's Evening' album for MCA, an indication that Taylor is still writing. If that's the case he could leap from obscurity to stardom. He has the talent.

Tin Star

From the same LA environment that threw up Dwight Yoakam and Rosie Flores, Tin Star have the potential to take progressive Californian country into the mainstream.

Led by guitarist Kerry Hansen, the band formed in 1984 with a desire to create an earthy, gutsy brand of country music. "We wanted to do something that harkened back to old-time country. We don't want to be part of that Nash-trash syndrome where everything is so overproduced. We want an edge to our music, that's what country is all about to me," says Hansen.

The band had a track on Enigma Records' 'A Town South Of Bakersfield' compilation album and then produced their own début album, 'Somebody's Dreams', which was later released in the UK on Special Delivery Records. Their music is rooted in old-time country as well as late sixties country rock. With luck the band should be more than a top flight local LA band.

Randy Travis

Once in a while an artist comes along who wipes the trophy case clean. Three years ago Travis was a struggling bar singer, in 1988 he's country music's most visible star, and at just 29 proof that country is no longer the property of the middle aged. He's sold over three million copies of his first two albums, won a brace of awards and managed to improve with every release. His low-key style, pure old-time country vocals and charming ingenuousness have made him an unlikely star, a symbol that when country music returned to basics it also threw away the spangled shirts, fancy dance steps and trite between-song chatter.

Travis, whose real name is Traywick, is a country boy, pure and simple. Born in Marshville, North Carolina, he grew up surrounded by country music. "Well I remember my daddy had all these old records, Hank Williams, Lefty Frizell, Ernest Tubb and old guys like that. I listened to them from when I was small." He started playing guitar aged just eight and by the tender age of 14 he and his brother were playing the local clubs.

A rebellious kid, he left home at 16 and lived the wild life for a while. "Hell! I was a real terror. I was in and out of jail and I'd get caught for drinking and drugs and stuff. These days I can't believe I was so wild. I hardly ever drink now."

Still he also had his music and at 16 he entered a talent show at Charlotte and won the contest easily. The club's owner Lib Hatcher gave him a regular spot which lasted for five years and Hatcher became so convinced of her protégé's talent that she sold up in 1981 and moved to Nashville. She became manager at the Nashville Palace and Travis worked regularly as Randy Ray, both as resident singer and short order cook.

For three years Lib Hatcher took his tapes to every label in town. Again and again they turned her down. "Well it bothered me that nothing seemed to be happening but I was enjoying myself and learning my craft, that was real important. I never got discouraged, you just have to wait for your time to come."

And come it did. In 1985 Hatcher dragged Warner Bros A&R Executive Martha Sharp to the club. Having seen the changes in country music, aware of George Strait's success and the move towards an almost nostalgic fifties-style country, Sharp listened to Travis' plaintive backwoods vocals with fresh ears. In 1985 Travis signed for Warner Bros, dropped the Randy Ray moniker, and thus began the most meteoric rise to the top in recent country history.

His first single for Warners was a Don Schlitz, Paul Overstreet tune, 'On The Other Hand' which fared only moderately, but his next effort, '1982', went to the top. On the strength of that, 'On The Other Hand' was re-released and naturally went to number one. The third single, 'Diggin' Up Bones', made it three in a row. Not a bad start. The album from which these hits were culled, 'Storms Of Life' (Warners) was one of the finest country débuts of all time.

Produced by Kyle Lehning it captured Travis' world-weary vocals perfectly. His hillbilly inflections were drawn out and the arrangements kept sparse but vital, a throwback to the best work of George Jones and Merle Haggard. When listeners discovered that the singer was not even 30-years-old, they lapped it up. Old timers liked it, young kids liked it and rock fans fell for Travis in a major way. The album went to the top of the charts and remained there for some months.

Touring commitments delayed the production of Travis' second album but when it came in 1987, 'Always And Forever' went on to make country music history as one of the fastest selling albums of all time. It also gave Travis four chart-topping singles,

notably 'Forever And Ever Amen' which won the 1987 Country Music Association award for single of the year. The album also won the corresponding album award, and Travis himself was selected as male vocalist of the year, a feat he repeated in 1988.

His third album, 'Old 8 By 10' (Warners) saw Travis again outselling his rivals and coming up with a slew of classic country songs. "We'll take a long time if necessary to get the right songs. We waited a long time for 'On The Other Hand' but once we found it it was certainly worth keeping."

Travis headlines shows these days, topping bills that include such stars as The Judds. He's come a long way fast but looks like he's learned the secret of longevity. He keeps out of the publicity spotlight, prefers the simple life to partying in town, and maintains a tightknit and loyal management team. He's not keen on the glitter and extravagance that often accompanies success. "Unlike some, I'm pretty much the same person off-stage as I am on. I'm definitely not a flashy dresser. I just want people to listen to the songs."

He's also investing wisely. Some of his royalties have been ploughed into a farm outside Nashville. When he's been on the road for months he has a local retreat, a place to recharge his rural batteries. He's also keen to improve his writing, if only he can find the time. "We're always so busy that I just don't seem to find the time to write. But it's something I do enjoy and I sure want to improve as a writer." If he writes as well as he sings and performs, he won't be needing Nashville's songwriters much longer.

Tanya Tucker

Country music has seen several child stars grace its stages over the years, but few have adapted with the times and trends and found new strengths and energies like Tanya Tucker. She's had more than 20 top 10 hits and at least nine number ones. These days she's riding the new country wave like a veteran with new heart.

Born in Seminole, Texas in 1958 Tucker spent her formative years in Phoenix Arizona, attending country music concerts with her star-struck father. Often Tucker would appear on-stage, the cute kid, with stars like Mel Tillis and Ernest Tubb. Her father took her to Nashville in a brand new Cadillac when she was just nine-years-old. Nothing happened but convinced Tanya had what it took to succeed in the entertainment business, her parents wangled the girl a small part in the cult western, *Jeremiah Johnson*.

Encouraged, they paid for her to cut a demo tape which found its way to Billy Sherrill who immediately signed her to CBS. She quickly recorded Alex Harvey's 'Delta Dawn' and achieved a top 10 hit. This was followed by hit songs, 'Blood Red And Going Down', 'Would You Lay With Me (In A Field Of Stone)'.

In 1976 she signed to MCA and continued to top the charts with singles from her MCA album, 'Here's Some Love'. In the early eighties Tucker attempted to move into the rock field with a sultry, sexy image and electric, hard-edged material. But things were falling apart. She endured an unhappy romance with Glen Campbell and began a comeback with Arista in 1982. But she was still outside the mainstream, still searching for a new direction. That came in 1986 when Tucker signed for Capitol and released two scorching albums, 'Girls Like Me' and 'Love Me Like You Used To' from which she scored another three number ones.

Her new sound reached near perfection on the 1988 album, 'Strong Enough To Bend' (Capitol). Produced by long-time associate Jerry Crutchfield, who Tucker trusts implicitly. "What makes Jerry a great producer is his willingness to try new

things," she says. "We've known each other for years and become great friends. That's half the battle right there." The album sounded fresh and uncluttered with Tucker's maturing vocals well up front. The material was spicy and contemporary drawing on writers like Don Schlitz and Lisa Silver. Interestingly she also proved she fully understood the sound of new country by recording an old Jimmie Rodgers tune, 'Daddy And Home' – a simple old-time tune brought bang up to date with Crutchfield and Tucker's treatment.

As the new breed of country artists threatens to overrun Nashville, artists like Tucker can only respond by quietly stepping aside, or reacting to the challenge. It seems Tucker has opted for the second option.

☆ ★ ★ ★ ☆

Ricky Van Shelton

A country artist with an ear for the traditional, Ricky Van Shelton is no spring chicken but 1987 and '88 have thrust him into the public eye, more than compensating for the years on the road paying music business dues.

Shelton grew up in a rural area of Virginia. His father, Jenks Shelton, was a part-time gospel musician and his love of music soon rubbed off on Ricky. When he first heard rock 'n' roll, Van Shelton was overcome. From the early sixties his passion was to be a musician. As a teenager he found country 'un-cool' preferring the rock music of The Beatles and The Rolling Stones. One night however, his older brother Ronnie and his bluegrass band asked Ricky to bring along his guitar and rapidly maturing baritone voice. Van Shelton wasn't impressed but went for the ride.

Once he heard the high lonesome sound first hand Ricky was a convert. He started listening to classic albums, played wherever he could and began writing his own songs. For several years Van Shelton learned his trade and only got close to stardom with the help of his wife Bettye who found a job in Nashville and supported Ricky while he concentrated on music. Months flew by and nobody liked his tapes. Fortunately Bettye's co-worker was Linda Thompson, wife of *The Tennesseean* newspaper's columnist Jerry Thompson. He was impressed by the tape and passed it on to friend Rick Blackburn at CBS. Blackburn attended a showcase at the Stockyard and brought along top producer Steve Buckingham.

Van Shelton's set included passionate versions of Ernest Tubb's 'Thanks A Lot' and Merle Haggard's 'Hungry Years', and within two weeks he was in the studio with Steve Buckingham working on recordings for CBS. Such was the speed of events that Van Shelton had no time to work on his own songs, so a series of classic numbers by Harlan Howard, Merle Haggard and Buck Owens were recorded in Van Shelton's unique manner. The album, 'Wild Eyed Dream' yielded three hit singles, the title track, 'Crime Of Passion' and 'Somebody Lied'.

For his next album, 'Living Proof', Van Shelton again worked with Buckingham, recording some classic country and his own tune, 'The Picture', which proved his talents as a writer were blossoming. Again the album had a solid sound, heavy drumming and rock 'n' roll back beats laced with wailing fiddles and taut steel guitar licks.

Van Shelton sings like a master, especially on the old Patsy Cline hit, 'He's Got You', which he updates with intelligence and subtlety. His live shows, thanks to years on the road, took little time to gel together. With a highly polished band and oodles of confidence, Van Shelton had audiences eating out of his hands around the United States. At the Fan Fair shindig of June 1987 he pulled a leg muscle and had to cancel his anticipated show.

But such was Van Shelton's appeal that fans begged his record company representatives to bring him to the signing booth. This they did and he arrived on a golf cart. "When I got to the booth there must have been 500 people there screaming and hollering. It was great. That really made Fan Fair for me. I must have signed 500 autographs that day." Already Shelton has a close relationship with his fans. His mix of old and new, honky tonk and rockabilly has taken him close to the top.

Townes Van Zandt

Best known in country circles as the writer of the frequently covered 'Pancho And Lefty', Van Zandt is an enigmatic figure hailed by some, especially Steve Earle, as a writing genius. Another Texan wordsmith, his songs are often off-the-wall but always hit hard and fast. His recording career has been patchy but it seems that he's about to enter a highly productive phase.

☆ ★ ★ ★ ☆

The Wagoneers

One of the youngest new country bands in years, The Wagoneers play tough country Texas-style, and have been signed by A&M Records, the company's first ever country signing. The band comprises Monte Warden, songwriter, singer and rhythm guitarist, bass player Craig Pettigrew and drummer Thomas Wilson. From the bar rooms of Austin, Texas where their rockabilly based country rock very quickly won them an army of supporters, to a recording studio in Nashville, the band's success has been rapid.

Formed in 1987 from various local bands, the individual members discovered they had similar interests in old-time country. Says Monte Warden, "We're not ashamed of country music. Country can be hard and exciting just like rock but it's also got a beauty that you just don't find anywhere else." They liked the sound of Buck Owens, Merle Haggard and of course Hank Williams. They also had a rockabilly influence from drummer Thomas Lewis who'd toured with former Sun records legend Sleepy La Beef.

Herb Alpert, the 'A' in A&M Records, played a major role in signing the band and even played trumpet on their début album, 'Stout And High' (A&M) in 1988. Produced by Emory Gordy Jr, the album was more mellow in tone than their live performances, concentrating more on the softer side of Monte Warden's considerable writing talents. They immediately won radio play, which surprised some, so wild was their reputation in Texas. Live they're still an awesome package; blistering twangy guitar, shuffling rhythms and inspired harmonies. The album recalls the beauty of Louvins and Everlys duets, the power of Ernest Tubb honky tonk and some of the more graceful elements of country rock.

Steve Wariner

More mainstream than some of his MCA labelmates, Wariner nonetheless has proved an enduring and talented Nashville newcomer. He began his musical career in the late seventies with a number of pop country releases, more recently MCA svengali Tony Brown has reshaped his sound, made it more country, and Wariner is reaping the benefits.

Born on Christmas Day 1954 in Kentucky, Wariner played bass in a country band before he reached his teens. He came to the attention of Chet Atkins at RCA who signed him and produced his early records. In 1984 he moved to MCA, was given more artistic freedom and moved smoothly with the times. His MCA album, 'One Good Night Deserves Another' was a breakthrough record and with his 1988 release, 'I Should Be With You' nestling into a long chart run he's firmly established as a gifted and versatile singer, writer and performer.

Keith Whitley

Whitley's death from alcohol abuse in the spring of 1989 was a tragic end to a promising career. One of the purest honky tonk singers in Nashville, Whitley had been knocking on the door of success for more years than he'd care to remember. He finally signed a deal with RCA in 1984 but his albums and singles didn't quite work, until his 1988 album, 'Don't Close Your Eyes', which finally captured his vocal talents in all their gravelly glory.

For a while Whitley had almost given up. Everyone had touted him as the next big thing ever since he was a child prodigy alongside Ricky Skaggs in the Ralph Stanley Band. But for some reason while all around him hit the headlines with their pure country approach, Whitley failed and instead hit the bottle. That he finally got it right in 1988 is testimony to his stamina and further proof that talent will eventually out.

From Sandy Hook, Kentucky, Whitley began playing music in a bluegrass band, soon teaming up with Ricky Skaggs in Ralph Stanley's Clinch Mountain Boys. In 1977 he joined JD Crowe And The New South, a bluegrass newgrass combo. The band won a vast following and Whitley led from the front, lead singer at just 21-years-old. He could do no wrong. But Whitley began to believe his publicity and when he moved to Nashville in 1984 expecting to be greeted as some kind of old timey conquering hero, he was instead greeted with indifference. Finally he persuaded RCA to give him a mini-album deal.

The six-song début, 'A Hard Act To Follow' (RCA) proved the complete opposite. If Whitley had followed that he'd have been in real trouble. Fortunately the next release, 'LA To Miami' yielded a few chart hits and it seemed that Whitley was adapting to the new-style Nashville.

Meanwhile he was having problems in his private life. He was drinking to excess, his brother Randy died in a motorcycle accident, his father passed away and he and his wife filed for divorce. Moreover RCA didn't have the confidence in their act that hindsight would have granted them.

Whitley recorded 'Does Fort Worth Ever Cross Your Mind' but RCA wouldn't release it. George Strait later took it to number one. His second album included 'On The Other Hand' and 'Nobody In His Right Mind Would've Left Her', but neither were released as singles. Randy Travis took the first to number one, George Strait the second. But Whitley kept going. He married *Grand Ole Opry* star Lorrie Morgan and they became parents in 1987.

Whitley thrived on the new responsibility, grew up fast and kicked the drinking habit. He saw clearly that his hard country sound was the key that would unlock the door of stardom. His third album, 'Don't Close Your Eyes' (RCA) saw Whitley capturing his live magic on vinyl. It was his finest moment. He covered Lefty Frizell's 'I Never Go Around Mirrors' with a cool, honky tonk power and roared through an up-tempo 'Flying Colors'. His band played their socks off and Whitley himself captured that back-to-basics vocal style perfectly.

Finally Whitley had established himself, a roots musician in the same mould as Randy Travis and George Strait but with a feel for both honky tonk and mountain music too.

CENTRE: WEBB WILDER

Webb Wilder And The Beatnecks

Wilder, a six-foot-four hillbilly in thirties detective gear is one of the most bizarre and original of Nashville's new acts. He calls his music, "hillbilly, gothic rock 'n' roll" and utilises a hard country band, off-the-wall lyrics and tongue in cheek humour. He'll happily cover a Hank Williams tune in his own way out style as the 'It Came From Nashville' album proves. (Landslide/Racket US, Special Delivery UK).

A left-field country artist who in many ways captures the spirit of Hank Williams, Wilder likes to take risks, and that can only be healthy for the development of country music.

Hank Williams Jr

He's been around since the early fifties but only since the seventies has Williams come out of his father's looming shadow and become a star in his own right. He was named the Country Music Association's Entertainer Of The Year in 1988. Hank Senior died when his son was just four-years-old and his mother was determined that Hank Jr would follow a music career in his father's wayward footsteps.

By the age of 16 he was a country music star, but he made his name from singing his father's tunes. Later in the seventies he scored with a string of mainstream country hits with a pop tinge. But he wasn't satisfied. According to his autobiography, *Living Proof* he was frustrated with the direction his career was taking. "They were polarised times and the music was the cutting edge of the times. If you listened to country music, you were a redneck and if you listened to rock 'n' roll you were a hippie freak. So what happened to the Allman Brothers in Macon, Georgia, was of no concern to the pickers in Nashville, Tennessee, just a couple of hundred miles up the road. But it was important to me because those Georgia boys were trying to tell me something."

In 1974 he moved from Nashville to Alabama and forged his southern country rock style. He almost died in a climbing accident in 1975 when he suffered serious head injuries, but he survived and put new energy into his music. In 1977 he moved from MGM to Warner Bros and finally had a top 20 hit in 1978 with 'I Fought The Law'.

Since then his rock-fired country has bubbled on several albums, notably 'Five-0' (Warners), 'Man Of Steel' (Warners) and his 1988 effort 'Wild Streak' (Warners). While many of his new country contemporaries are harking back to the fifties, Williams is looking to the future. He's been playing progressive country for a decade and is probably the most powerful performer in country music.

☆　★　★　★　☆

Lori Yates

Canadian born singer Lori Yates made a name for herself in her home town of Toronto before taking on the country establishment in Nashville. At 17 she was absorbing herself in country music and writing songs in the booth of the gas station where she worked. She found a band, Rang Tang, in the autumn of 1986 and quickly won good reviews across the board in Toronto. They made a single, 'Sweetheart Avenue' but it was never released. Fortunately someone at CBS heard the song and Yates signed to the company in 1987.

She has recorded tracks with the legendary Bob Johnston who produced 'Blonde On Blonde' and 'Nashville Skyline' for Bob Dylan. She's also cut tracks with Sweethearts Of The Rodeo producer Steve Buckingham. Both men were struck by the ferocity of her delivery and deep country timbre of her vocals. A début album awaits release.

Dwight Yoakam

Probably the hippest new country act and certainly the most outspoken, Yoakam's brash militance caught the imagination of the rock press and rock fans and his role in taking country to a newer, younger audience has been vital. He has scored with three impressive albums and sell-out tours, including several with fifties West Coast legend Buck Owens.

From Pikeville, Kentucky, he grew up with country music. "I lived in hillbilly country. Country music was all around – you know Hank Williams, Bill Monroe. I started singing Ralph Stanley kinda songs and in high school I had a rockabilly band." He tried pop and rock for a while but soon realised that country was his real calling. "It was like an ill-fitting suit doing pop for me. I figured that if I loved that old Stonewall Jackson sound then there'd probably be other people who did too.

In the mid-seventies Yoakam came to Nashville. He wasn't appreciated. "They didn't like my music, said it was too country. How can it be too country for Christ sake? Those record executives had lost sight of the real country music, Hank Williams, Roy Acuff and Bill Monroe, the people that built that town."

Dismayed and hurt, Yoakam relocated to Los Angeles. Instead of playing country bars with cover versions he put together a tough honky tonk band and played to rock audiences. "I gave up good money in the country bars. It wasn't easy. We weren't immediately embraced by the young people of LA. Helped along by LA roots bands Los Lobos and The Blasters, Yoakam found himself gigs, gradual acceptance and eventual appreciation. He was convinced that hard-edged country music would appeal to rock fans. "I want people to see the links. Hank Williams was the predecessor of rock 'n' roll."

Yoakam recorded a track for the seminal, 'A Town South Of Bakersfield' album on Enigma. Producer Pete Anderson was impressed and together they recorded a mini-album which so impressed Warners that it became Yoakam's début release, 'Guitars, Cadillacs Etc Etc'. "We tried for the same kind of echo that you hear on Stonewall Jackson records. I mean we used up to the minute technology. I'm not a revivalist but we did want to recapture that old sound."

The album caused a stir in Nashville. Thanks to his base of support as a live act it sold well and won radio play, it seemed that Nashville would welcome Yoakam back as a star. Unfortunately some comments he made in the British press about 'Nash-trash' and some slurs on producers and executives cast him as the black sheep of the country family. That image probably didn't harm his commercialism, especially in the rock market, but Yoakam was never a complete outsider, never the foul mouthed rebel he was painted. In 1987 he told *Spin* magazine how his support of various aspects of the Nashville set up failed to make the press.

His second album, 'Hillbilly Deluxe', was not as dynamic as his début but it charted well and spent over 70 weeks in the *Billboard* chart. He toured to great effect, winning much support from rock fans, especially in England where he became something of a cult hero. The album again concentrated on a fifties style, a kind of music first played by Buck Owens. Yoakam called it, "Bill Monroe meets Hank Williams plus drums." His idea for 'Hillbilly Deluxe' was that it would continue in the same vein as the first album but with added polish and finesse. "We took the cream off 'Guitar, Cadillacs Etc Etc' and built it from there. I hope that people feel the innocence of that first record and I hope they can pick up on the polish and enthusiasm of the new one."

Yoakam toured Stateside with his idol Buck Owens, who popped up as a guest on Yoakam's 1988 album, 'Buenos Noches From A Lonely Room' (Warners). The record built on the other two, the sound was fuller, Yoakam's vocals more assured and the songs tighter. He mixed up the rhythms, utilised top rate players like Tom Brumley and Al Perkins and added a nice touch with some Mexican flourishes. Yoakam had proved his worth, proved his affection for country music and as a side effect brought Buck Owens out of retirement and into a new deal with Capitol.

☆ ★ ★ ★ ☆

UK COUNTRY

Despite the fact that the traditional folk music of England, Scotland and Ireland formed the core of country music in the States, no UK acts have managed to threaten the premiership of American country music. With country looking back to its roots, it is possible that UK artists, a little closer to the original roots, may come up with a dynamic new approach to rival the likes of Strait and Yoakam. As yet much of the UK's country output is stuck in the mainstream rather than the adventurous. There are some optimistic signs however.

Throughout the late seventies and eighties two artists, Wes McGhee and Hank Wangford, led the progressive country sound in England. Wangford, a London gynaecologist, met Gram Parsons in the early seventies and inspired by his country rock example put his own band together. With a sound boosted by a host of top session players, Wangford made a classy, country rock-style début album for the small Cow Pie label in the early eighties. However his predilection for scathing sarcasm moved him more towards a cabaret and theatre environment rather than developing a serious country image. Wangford has become a London celebrity and hosted TV shows on country music but has still to recapture the promise of his early musical efforts.

One of the players on Wangford's self-titled début album was Albert Lee, a virtuoso guitarist, who has surrounded himself with accolades and earned a reputation as the finest country guitar player to come out of Britain. He played with Chet Atkins back in 1969 but really came into his own as guitarist with Emmylou Harris's Hot Band.

Albert, an affable, easy going fellow who is liked in the industry and disarmingly modest about his extraordinary talents, went on to play in Eric Clapton's band and with the reformed Everly Brothers in the eighties. His composition 'Country Boy', originally recorded when he played in Heads, Hands And Feet, is among the most endearing British country songs and the tune often gets an airing when Albert is on-stage – regardless of his employer at the time. The song also became a hit for Ricky Skaggs.

These days he's always in demand, plays the odd solo show and has released some instrumental works for the exciting MCA Masters series. He has also produced a brilliant instructional video for budding country pickers as part of the Starlicks series.

Wes McGhee, a veteran of pub rock bands of the sixties, became involved in country music in the seventies after building a studio in his house in which he absorbed himself in Texas country music. These days he's as well respected in the States as any American artist. He regularly tours the US with a band that includes Joe Ely, drummer Freddy Krc and noted accordionist Ponty Bone. He's also made a series of progressive albums, notably 'Airmail' and 'Landing Lights'. A new 'best of' collection will be released in 1989 by London's fledgling PT Records.

OPPOSITE:
ALBERT LEE
BELOW:
WES MCGHEE

115

McGhee made history in 1988 as the first British-based artist to be signed to a Nashville publishing company as a writer. If Bug Music do their stuff, and Nashville Director Gary Valetri is as keyed in as anyone in country music, then McGhee's songs should start being recorded in Nashville.

In 1981 Elvis Costello made significant steps towards legitimising country music in the UK by releasing 'Almost Blue', an album of country standards recorded in Nashville with producer Billy Sherrill. Though the experiment was not entirely successful, the fact that a critically respected rock musician like Costello, a man known for his uncompromising music, should record country songs was a pointer to the music's gradual mainstream acceptance in the eighties. Costello followed up the LP with a concert at London's Royal Albert Hall at which he performed many of the 'Almost Blue' songs with the Royal Philharmonic Orchestra. It was a prestigious occasion attended by many of the rock cognoscenti.

In the eighties, after a brief explosion of punk-based country bands, (labelled cowpunk by *The Sunday Times*) progressive country music faded somewhat. An enterprising duo, The Panic Brothers, won a sizeable following on the live circuit with a collection of witty, high energy country-based songs and recorded an album for new London country label, Special Delivery (a division of folk music legends Topic Records). 'In The Red' won great reviews but their music was a little ahead of its time for the UK.

At the time of writing, two, as yet unsigned, UK artists are threatening to cause a stir. Terry Clarke plays Texas-based country rock and has a healthy following on the live club scene. A cheaply produced demo tape by singer and songwriter Jo Knights has gained the attention of several music journalists and suggests that the art of complex song arrangements, insightful lyrics and heartfelt vocals is not limited to Nashville or Texas.

☆ ★ ★ ★ ☆

CLASSIC/COUNTRY

While late eighties country music may have opened itself to a diversity of styles and influences, the impetus of the new changes in Nashville was definitely the new traditionalist trend. Ricky Skaggs was so influenced by Bill Monroe that he invited him on to his 'Country Boy' video; Dwight Yoakam toured with fifties legend Buck Owens and drew inspiration from Owens, Hank Williams and Stonewall Jackson; Nanci Griffith was inspired by the music of Woody Guthrie and Loretta Lynn; Randy Travis and George Strait base their style on Merle Haggard, Lefty Frizell and George Jones.

These then are some of the key figures in classic country, figures who have directly influenced the new wave of eighties country artists.

Roy Acuff

Known as The King Of Country, Roy Acuff is the grand old man of Nashville. Born in 1903 he made his first appearance on the Opry in 1938, a popular act with his down-home mountain boy approach. In 1942 he and Fred Rose set up the Acuff-Rose publishing company which became one of the most important in country music. Acuff had big hits during the war years, notably 'Wreck On The Highway'. In 1962 he was honoured as a member of the Country Music Hall Of Fame. In 1972 he guested on The Nitty Gritty Dirt Band's generation spanning classic album, 'Will The Circle Be Unbroken?' Greatest Hits collections are available on the Elektra and Columbia labels.

Chet Atkins

Perhaps the most famous of all Nashville musicians, Chet Atkins moved to music city as a singer but it was his instrumental work that found him fame and fortune. He was top session guitarist for RCA in the forties, moved to A&R in 1952 and became a Vice President of the company in 1968. He's credited with creating the famous Nashville Sound and produced hit records for scores of musicians, including Elvis Presley. Atkins has always been one of the more open-minded establishment figures with the result that many new country artists treat him with great respect and seek his wisdom and advice.

OPPOSITE:
HANK WILLIAMS

119

The Carter Family

Right at the bedrock of country in the early years were The Carter Family who are still performing in various formats. A.P. Carter, the dominant figure in the early days, introduced old folk songs into his family's repertoire, and they became known for tunes like, 'Wildwood Fire' and 'Keep On The Sunnyside'. The family made historic early recordings for RCA and worked consistently through the Great Depression finally breaking up in 1943.

Maybelle Carter (wife of A.P.'s brother), a fine and innovative guitarist, formed a group with her three daughters but June eventually left to marry and work with Johnny Cash. Eventually all the members of The Carter Family joined the Cash roadshow and remain with them today. Maybelle Carter also appeared on The Nitty Gritty Dirt Band's, 'Will The Circle Be Unbroken?' album. '20 Of The Best' (RCA) is as good an introduction to The Carter Family's backwoods, folk and country music as any.

Johnny Cash

Born in 1932 in Arkansas, Johnny Cash has been one of the most enduring and charismatic country stars of the past 30 years. A contemporary of Elvis at Sun Records, he went on to become the much loved 'Man In Black', a deep gravelly voiced story teller famed for his support of the downtrodden. He met up with Luther Perkins and Marshall Grant in 1954 and played with them on KWEM radio station. They won a deal with Sun and recorded 'Hey Porter/Cry Cry Cry', an immediate hit. The follow-up, 'Folsom Prison Blues' was also a hit and Cash became a star.

Since then he's made films, been a folk music hero in the sixties, a protester for civil rights, a Bob Dylan champion, abused his body with drink and drugs, written his own version of the Gospel, been elected to the Country Music Hall Of Fame and become one of the best known performers in the world. His sparse, bass vocals and choppy guitar became a trademark, copied by many, equalled by none.

Patsy Cline

Possibly the most famous female country singer of the fifties, her version of Willie Nelson's 'Crazy' is still the best and her recordings with producer Owen Bradley set new standards for country records. She was important in leading a country attack on the pop charts and, had she not died young, it's certain she would have been the biggest star of them all.

The Everly Brothers

Don and Phil may have achieved Las Vegas and pop success in later years but to begin with they were pure Kentucky country. 'Bye Bye Love' was their first hit, an introduction to their high soaring harmonies, booming acoustic guitars and lyrics that dealt with teenage love. Further hits included 'Wake Up Little Susie', 'All I Have To Do Is Dream', 'Bird Dog' and many more. They recorded for Cadence with Chet Atkins behind the desk but left their Nashville base in 1960, gradually developing a more rock and pop sound.

Flatt And Scruggs

Alongside Bill Monroe with whom they worked, Flatt And Scruggs were probably the best known bluegrass act in America. After many years of acclaim they achieved national celebrity in 1962 with the theme tune from *The Beverly Hillbillies* but in fact they had been working together since 1948.

Flatt, a singer and guitarist noted for his 'G run', and Scruggs all but revolutionised banjo playing. They were both interested in pushing bluegrass forward and with Monroe very much a purist they went out on their own with the Foggy Mountain Boys, and began recording for Mercury. They used less mandolin and more banjo and they championed a fast, driving bluegrass. In 1949 they recorded 'Foggy Mountain Breakdown' which was later used to great effect in the movie *Bonnie And Clyde*.

In the fifties Flatt And Scruggs moved to Columbia and became more established in straight country circles. They played on the *Martha White Biscuit Time* on Nashville's WSM radio and eventually its TV equivalent. In the sixties the folk revival saw them in demand and Scruggs in particular thrived on the experimental music of the time. Flatt preferred the traditional sound and they split in 1969.

Earl Scruggs played a major role on the 'Will The Circle Be Unbroken?' album for The Dirt Band and still plays the odd breakneck banjo lick on country records. Lester Flatt died in 1979.

Lefty Frizzell

Famed honky tonker from the fifties, the big man (he was also a useful boxer) started his Capitol career with 'If You've Got The Money, I've Got The Time' and later hit the top with 'Always Late' and 'Mom And Dad's Waltz'. He died in 1975.

Woody Guthrie

Famed for his folk/country tunes documenting the plight of migrants in the Depression, Woody Guthrie has influenced countless musicians down the years. His 'Dust Bowl Ballads' (Folkways) is a marvellous and moving account of human tragedy for Guthrie is never afraid to point an accusing finger at authority. A slogan on his guitar read, 'This guitar kills fascists' and he found himself threatened by Government agencies for his outspoken views. Guthrie suffered from Huntington's chorea from the mid-fifties until 1967 when he died.

Bob Dylan made a pilgrimage to Woody's bedside and is his most famous devotee, though Bruce Springsteen often sings a moving version of 'This Land Is Your Land' in concert. The song, perhaps Woody's most famous anthem, was written in response to Irving Berlin's 'God Bless America'.

Merle Haggard

Still going strong, Merle Haggard maintained a honky tonk vision when others opted for a softer country sound. Haggard was in San Quentin prison serving a sentence for burglary when Johnny Cash performed there in 1960 and when he left the same year he opted for a music career.

Based in Bakersfield, California, which had a growing country music community, Haggard had his first number one in 1966 with 'The Fugitive' (Capitol). He penned the redneck anthems 'Okie From Muskogee' and 'The Fightin' Side Of Me' but he was never an out and out reactionary, more a spokesman of the people. Since the sixties he's become a superstar but his early recordings with their mix of honky tonk, swing and dusty ballads strengthened country music's links with its past.

Stonewall Jackson

Named after the Confederate General, Jackson went to Nashville in 1956 and found immediate success. His massive hit 'Waterloo' (Columbia) pushed him to international standing and he even appeared on Dick Clark's *Bandstand*. A 'Greatest Hits' album on Columbia is testimony to the man's honky tonk finesse.

George Jones

Jones has for a long time been *the* voice in country music. In latter days he opted for an easy-going crooning style but in the beginning Jones played hard, rockabilly-tinged country music. Countless hits followed his breakthrough tune, 'Why Baby Why', including 'She Thinks I Still Care', 'If My Heart Had Windows' and many more. In the late sixties he mellowed his style, embracing the Nashville sound and style, and for a long time recorded with Tammy Wynette. He's still going strong, probably the finest singer in country music.

125

CHARLIE LOUVIN

The Louvin Brothers

Ira and Charlie were one of the best country music duos of all time. Their peak came in the fifties with a slew of records that portrayed their close harmony vocals. In 1955 they became Opry regulars but they parted in 1962. Ira died a year later but Charlie continues to play and sing. Rounder Records have a series of Louvins albums available, notably 'The Louvin Brothers'.

Loretta Lynn

Loretta Lynn's story became internationally known after the success of the biographical movie *A Coalminer's Daughter*. From a mining community in Kentucky, she formed a band in the fifties and recorded her first hit 'Honky Tonk Girl' in 1960. She and her husband, toured the country with the record and finally The Wilburn Brothers asked Loretta to join them in Nashville.

After she broke into the charts in 1962 with 'Success' she became a prolific hit maker and a country superstar. Importantly she began writing songs from a woman's point of view including, 'Don't Come Home A Drinkin'', 'Woman Of The World', 'One's On The Way'. Later she recorded 'The Pill' a breakthrough song for liberalising country music attitudes.

Monroe Brothers

Bill and Charlie, together and separately, practically invented bluegrass music. They played traditional Kentucky music in the thirties and won radio work as the Monroe Brothers. Even then their vocals rang high and true and the mandolin sound was well to the fore. In 1938 they parted and Bill went on to work with his Bluegrass Boys, eventually picking up banjo expert Earl Scruggs in 1945 and honing his distinctive bluegrass style.

In 1949 he signed to Decca and worked with singer Jimmy Martin and enjoyed a period of great success, recording classics like 'Uncle Pen' and 'Walkin' In Jerusalem' (both covered by Ricky Skaggs). Bluegrass, fiddle and banjo dominated music with high lonesome vocals declined through the rock 'n' roll era but made a major comeback in the sixties folk revival. Monroe continues to play a hard driving mountain sound.

ABOVE:
BILL MONROE
BELOW LEFT:
BUCK OWENS
(CENTRE) **AND HIS**
BUCKAROOS

Patsy Montana

Notable as the first woman in country music to hit a million sales on a single, 'I Want To Be A Cowboy's Sweetheart' in 1935.

Buck Owens

Buck Owens is the voice and inspiration behind the Californian Bakersfield sound. He and his band the Buckaroos began a series of successful recordings in 1959 and Owens had 17 number ones between 1963 and 1969 including, 'Act Naturally', 'Buckaroo' and 'I've Got A Tiger By The Tail' for Capitol. In 1976 he left Capitol for Warners but couldn't recapture his former top 10 glories. However with Dwight Yoakam championing the Owens style and dragging him out of retirement in 1988, Owens is still a force in country music.

Jimmie Rodgers

Rodgers was probably the first country music star, famous for his railroad songs and blues yodelling. Rodgers recorded for RCA in the late twenties and thirties and his combination of folk, blues and country made him a household name. Even throughout the Depression fans bought his records by the million, and songs like, 'Brakeman's Blues', 'T For Texas' and 'Mother Was A Lady' proved immensely popular. Sadly, ill health shortened Rodgers' musical career and he died from TB in a recording studio in New York at the age of 29. RCA's '20 Of The Best' is a perfect example of his 12-bar blues and country style.

Ernest Tubb

Ernest Tubb was a regular on the Opry from 1943 until his death. He brought an electric honky tonk sound to country music and though he was never a great singer, his recordings sold in their millions. 'Walking The Floor Over You' in 1942 was his first hit and he was a consistent hit maker through the fifties. Tubb was always a prolific tourer and he and his band The Troubadours played more than 300 dates a year.

Hank Williams

Country music, however magical and innovative it was, remained in Hicksville until the arrival of Hank Williams. A pale, lanky man, he commanded great stage presence and a songwriting ability that has never been matched. He and his Drifting Cowboys band played for radio shows through the forties, signing for MGM in 1947. An alcoholic, he nevertheless worked for the *Louisiana Hayride* show and with the success of 'Lovesick Blues' became an Opry regular.

He cut top 10 hits with amazing regularity including, 'Mind Your Own Business', 'You're Gonna Change', 'My Bucket's Got A Hole In It', 'Jambalaya, 'Kaw Liga' and 'I'll Never Get Out Of This World Alive'. Drugs and alcohol, together with a back ailment suffered since childhood, brought about his demise but his records and influence on country music was mammoth. His songs were among the first country tunes to be covered by pop artists and there's hardly a new country act who hasn't been inspired by Hank The Great.

HANK WILLIAMS

Bob Wills

Known as the King Of Western Swing, Wills led his Texas Playboys through the pre-war years, fusing country and dance music long before rock 'n' roll achieved a similar feat. From 1929 to 1973 he made over 550 recordings but he's still best known for his 'San Antonio Rose'.

☆　★　★　★　☆